WHAT'S THE BIG IDEA?

Inventions that Changed Life on Earth Forever

MAPLE TREE PRESS

Helaine Becker

Illustrated by Steve Attoe

Maple Tree Press books are published by Owlkids Books Inc.
10 Lower Spadina Avenue, Suite 400, Toronto, Ontario M5V 2Z2
www.owlkids.com

Distributed in Canada by Raincoast Books
9050 Shaughnessy Street, Vancouver, British Columbia V6P 6E5

Distributed in the United States by Publishers Group West
1700 Fourth Street, Berkeley, California 94710

Dedication
To kids everywhere—tomorrow's innovators and inventors

Acknowledgments
Holly Dunsworth, Northeastern Illinois University; Clemens Reichel, University of
Toronto; Jesse Kapp, University of Toronto; Andrew Iarocci - Collections Manager,
Transportation & Artillery, Canadian War Museum; Dr. Jaymie Matthews, Astronomy
Undergraduate Advisor, Department of Physics & Astronomy, University of British
Columbia; thanks to the Ontario Arts Council for their financial support through the
Writers' Reserve program.

Library and Archives Canada Cataloguing in Publication

Becker, Helaine, 1961-
    What's the big idea? : inventions that changed life on
earth forever / Helaine Becker ; illustrated by Steve Attoe.

ISBN 978-1-897349-60-1 (bound).--ISBN 978-1-897349-61-8 (pbk.)

    1. Inventions--Juvenile literature. I. Attoe, Steve II. Title.

T48.B42 2009   j609   C2009-901001-1

Library of Congress Control Number: 2009923330

Design: Barb Kelly; Word & Image Design Studio

 Canada Council   Conseil des Arts    ONTARIO ARTS COUNCIL
for the Arts   du Canada   CONSEIL DES ARTS DE L'ONTARIO

We acknowledge the financial support of the Canada Council for the Arts, the Ontario
Arts Council, the Government of Canada through the Book Publishing Industry
Development Program (BPIDP), and the Government of Ontario through the Ontario
Media Development Corporation's Book Initiative for our publishing activities.

Printed in China

A   B   C   D   E   F

CONTENTS

Introduction   4

Long, Long Ago...   6
Needle   8
Wheel   10
Plow   12
Water Pump   14
Big Thinkers:
    Archimedes   16
Alphabet   18
Close-up:
    At School   20
Spinning Wheel   22
Compass   24
Paper   26
Close-up:
    In the Bathroom   28

Long Ago...   30
Printing Press   32
Big Thinkers:
    Leonardo da Vinci   34
Lenses   36
Accurate Clock   38
Steam Engine   40
Steel   42
Electric Battery   44
Food Canning   46
Close-up:
    At War   48
Photograph   50
Electric Motor   52
Big Thinkers:
    Michael Faraday   54
Telegraph   56
Fertilizer   58
Light Bulb   60
Close-up:
    In the Doctor's Office 62

Not So Long Ago...   64
Engine   66
Car   68
Telephone   70
Big Thinkers:
    Alexander Graham Bell   72
Radio   74
Television   76
Airplane   78
Plastic   80
Close-up:
    In the Kitchen   82
Computer   84
Personal Computer   86
Big Thinkers:
    Steve Jobs & Bill Gates 88
Internet   90
MP3   92

What's Next?   94
Index   96

Coming up with **new ideas** is easy. **Getting them to work** is a different story.

When I sat down to write this book, I was inspired by one cool, weird fact: Bicycles were invented, in part, because of a massive 1815 volcano eruption in Indonesia. It made me want to know what other unexpected events had led to major inventions. Was there a link, perhaps, between ancient Chinese warfare and paper napkins? Or wine-making and printed books?

The answer to both questions is YES. You see, every invention starts with a simple need. Maybe you need to protect yourself from scary strangers. So you invent armor. Or perhaps you're sick of lugging around your stuff in a smelly buffalo hide. So you invent wagons or backpacks. Maybe you need a way to get around after bad weather—caused by a faraway volcanic eruption—has killed your horses. So you invent...the bicycle.

As you read this book, you might wonder a few things. Like, where are all the women inventors? And what about Asians, or Africans, or aboriginal peoples? Why are so many of these inventors turning out to be dead white guys? There *are* reasons for these things. First off, in the olden days, women everywhere got a raw deal. They wound up coming up with plenty of inventions, but men took the credit for them. Secondly, the white men of Western Europe weren't smarter or more talented than other people. They had just gotten lucky. Thanks to a fluke of geography and history, for hundreds of years Europe wound up being the place to be if you wanted to develop new ideas.

Speaking of new ideas, this book is just the tip of invention's iceberg—there are so many more kooky tidbits to discover. Maybe I couldn't squeeze in every fantasta-fact out there, like how ancient Romans used pee to make toothpaste, but that doesn't mean you can't track them down yourself. (Check out my website for some leads, www.helainebecker.com.) I hope this book whets your appetite for innovation and sends you searching for more examples on your own (like how whalers made raincoats).

Happy Hunting,

Helaine

I'm Hungry
I need to obtain, cook, and store food.

The Six Basic Needs

Innovation—the ability to come up with new ideas and use familiar objects in new ways—is something that makes us unique in the animal kingdom. It's allowed us to invent everything from soap to steel, telephones to toilets, compasses to computers. In fact, the most incredible inventions of all time— the ones that literally changed our world—have all burst forth to meet one of these six basic needs:

I'm Cold and Wet
I need protection from the weather.

I'm Tired
I need to reduce the amount of physical work required to do a job or travel.

5

Long, Long, Long Ago...

From Hunter to Farmer

Long, long ago, all human beings were hunter-gatherers living in small tribes. Life was simple, but death could strike in an instant. You could be attacked by animals, or weakened by starvation, exposure, or infection.

Our ancestors lived like this for millions of years. Then, about ten thousand years ago, people in Mesopotamia came up with a less risky way of living: They learned to herd goats and sheep so they no longer needed dangerous hunts. They also figured out how to grow their crops so they could have a ready supply of nutritious grains.

These innovations had more far-reaching effects than any Mesopotamian shepherd could imagine. Cities grew, and with them came governments, trade, mathematics, and writing. Not all changes were positive. Government also led to tyrants, taxes, and even slavery. Great wealth for some meant poverty for others. People living in close quarters saw increased disease and shorter life spans.

But many inventions truly made life easier. Ships for transportation by water, wheels for travel by land, iron for plows to till the soil, and pumps to water fields all began to appear. Soon, human life looked nothing like our old hunter-gatherer days—we were farming the land.

It's cold. It's wet. And that leaf you're wearing is awfully drafty. What you need is a...

NEEDLE

The first clothing was probably a honking-big leaf draped over someone's head like a rain bonnet. Animal skins were also used as quickie coverings. There was just one tiny problem—they didn't exactly fit. Sometimes you could tie strips of skin around you, but that didn't always work either.

HIGHLIGHTS Invented by: Damp, depressed and very chilly wome

The Lowdown on Leather

Fresh animal skins smell—yuck—like dead animals. The first fashion fad was treating the stinky skins to make them smell better. One popular method was to soak them in—double-yuck—pee! Treating the skins this way also made them softer and longer-lasting.

Needle Knows

A sharp-thinking cave dweller realized she could poke holes along the edge of an animal skin. She could then attach it to another skin by looping stretchy tendons or leather thongs through the holes.

Poking the holes and lacing the leather was slow work. It was tough to make fitted, comfy pieces of clothing (like undies). About forty thousand years ago, new types of needles appeared on the scene. They were made of bone or ivory. They had holes, called eyes, punched through the top. The eyes let clothing makers use just one tool—and a single motion—to poke the hole and draw the lacing through. An eyed needle also meant that you could make teensy-weensy holes and use very fine threads, like horsehair. It also meant that the art of sewing was born.

SPINOFFS

The first **socks** came into vogue around 800 BCE in Greece. They were probably made from felt.

Buttons were used by the ancient Greeks to help keep their clothes in place. Button holes, however, weren't invented until much, much later! (The Greeks used button loops.)

Bikinis first appeared in wall paintings dating back to 1600 BCE. The modern bikini was invented in 1945 and named after—of all things—an atomic bomb test site, Bikini Atoll, in the Pacific Ocean.

According to legend, **silk** was invented in 2600 BC by 14-year-old Lei-Tzu, who was also a Chinese empress. Lei-Tzu was sipping tea under a mulberry tree one day when a cocoon of the *Bomybx mori* moth dropped into her cup. When the cocoon began to unravel in the hot tea, the empress had the long fiber woven into a beautiful, durable fabric. That fabric was silk. Lei-Tzu is also credited as the inventor of the loom in China.

You're All Stitched Up!

Well-fitting clothing meant that people could live in many more parts of the world, especially colder climates. Some researchers think that, thanks to some superbly tailored animal skin pants and jackets, our ancestors were able to survive the Ice Age while the poor needle-less Neanderthals could not.

When: 40,000 years ago   **Where: Parts of what is today called Russia**

Clay pots sure are big business in the ancient world—too bad yours are all covered with your ugly thumbprints! Maybe it's time for a new spin on pottery...

WHEEL

Believe it or not, the first wheel was not used for getting around. It was invented by pottery makers! They realized that if they placed clay on a platform, and balanced the platform on a pebble, they could rotate the platform. They could then mold pots smoothly, without picking them up.

Once the wheel was invented, it wasn't long before people got around to using it in other ways.

HIGHLIGHTS Invented by: No one wheely knows   When: About 2700 BC

The first **spoked wheels** appeared on chariots around 1600 BCE. Large, spoked wheels let chariots travel much faster over bumpy ground—a big plus during battle. Not so bad for your bike either.

Turns out, wheels are needed to make **gears** and **pulleys** work. Today, these simple machines can be found in almost any device you can name. Like what? Well, clocks, pumps, motors, and computers, for starters!

Rolling Down the River

Before stone-paved roads—which didn't appear until about 4000 BCE—wheeled vehicles would have been more trouble than help. Besides, people could carry their few possessions fairly easily. Larger loads traveled in boats along rivers. When people had to move a heavy load over land, they just placed it on top of several large logs. The logs acted as rollers, and were moved from the back to the front as needed. Sometimes runners, like those on a sled, were placed under the load to move it more smoothly.

Around 2700 BCE, someone got the revolutionary idea of putting wheels, instead of runners, on the load. The only problem was how to attach the wheels. The first solution was to stick the wheels to an axle. Both the wheels and axle turned together. That was okay, but it was hard to go around corners without tipping. The improved version had a fixed axle that let the wheels spin around it.

The first wheels were cut from wooden slabs. They were heavy and not very strong. Gradually, people learned to cut holes in the wheels to make them both stronger and lighter.

They Set the Future in Motion

Wheels are used today on everything from scooters to SUVs—they are even used on the space shuttle! Even more than just getting us from one place to another, the idea of the wheel influenced nearly every mechanical device in history.

Where: Mesopotamia (in what is now known as Iraq)

So, you got down on your hands and knees, loosened the soil with your fingers and stuffed the seeds into the dirt. That was waaaay too much work.

You need a tool to make planting easier, something like a...

PLOW

To loosen the soil, the first successful farmers dragged pointy digging sticks along the ground. Sometimes the points were hardened by heating them in fire or tipping them with stone. Eventually, the digging sticks evolved into a simple tool called an ard. It had a sharpened blade for cutting the soil, a handle for guiding its path, and a long shaft for farmers to pull.

HIGH**LIGHTS** Invented by: Some tired, cranky farmers   When: About 350

The Ox Rocks!

By 3500 BCE, people in the Middle East realized that if they could get strong animals to pull the plows, spring planting would be a snap. So they came up with a way to hitch oxen to it. Snap! This was probably the first time in history that animal power was used for labor.

Plowing Ahead

In the third century BCE, the Chinese came up with a terrific plow called a "kuan." It had a blade shaped something like a butterfly. The blade's sharp point dug into the ground, while its "wings" threw dirt off to the side, turning it over and burying weeds.

But the efficient butterfly design did not reach Europe for another two thousand years. There, from the Middle Ages until the nineteenth century, the design of the plow barely changed. Europe's plows were heavy and required oxen or horses to pull them through the dense soil.

Breathe Easy

Speaking of horses, they were great at pulling—way stronger than oxen. Horse-loving farmers in the Middle Ages had just one little problem. The harnesses went right across their poor pony's windpipe. Choke! Around 900 CE, a better harness, called the horse collar, arrived in Europe from China. Hard-working horsies across the continent breathed a lot easier.

Steel Yourself for More Innovation

In 1837, American blacksmith John Deere introduced the steel plow. The steel blade was much stronger than previous ones. It let people settle areas that had never been suitable for farming, like the American prairies. The U.S. was able to grow dramatically after the steel plow was introduced.

That's One Plow-erful Invention

The plow enabled the world's first farmers to make a living from the land. This, in turn, allowed people to settle down in one place instead of all that hunting and gathering. Bingo! You've got yourself the basis for modern civilization.

13

So you want to be a farmer, do you?
It's hard work—one failed crop and your whole family starves.
The first step is watering your fields so your crops don't flop.

WATER PUMP

The shadouf was the first invention that made irrigation easier. On one end was a leather bucket. On the other was a weight. To operate the shadouf, you pushed down on the pole to plunk the bucket into the water. Then you let go. The counterweight lifted the full bucket into the air. The bucket could then be emptied into an irrigation ditch.

The shadouf worked so well, in fact, that it remained the only water pump used throughout the Middle East for more than two thousand years.

Somewhere in the Middle East (possibly as early as 200 BCE), the noria was invented. It was a large wheel with pails fixed all around the edge, like a Ferris wheel. As a river flowed through it, the wheel turned. The pails would get dunked and lifted one by one as the wheel moved. Each water-laden bucket could then be dumped into an irrigation ditch.

A later improvement on the noria, the saqiya, used horses or oxen to power the pump. It also used wheels as gears.

The Big Step Up

In 600 BCE, King Nebuchadnezzar of Babylon built the Hanging Gardens, a mountain-sized garden known as one of the Seven Wonders of the World. Just how did he water this? No one knows for sure, but here are three possibilities:

1. Archimedes' Screw

Greek mathematician Archimedes slid a giant screw inside a hollow tube. One end was stuck in the water. When the screw was turned, its spiral grooves carried water around and around, up the tube and out the top! Neat, except that he lived about three hundred years *after* Nebuchadnezzar. Some experts think a version of this device had already been invented before Archimedes.

2. The Chain Pump

Take two large wheels. Place one above the other. Connect the wheels with a rope loop. Hang buckets along the rope. Turn the top wheel using a crank. As the wheel turns, buckets dip into a pool and pick up water. The loop then lifts them to the upper wheel, where the buckets can be dumped into a higher pool.

3. The Force Pump

A solid tube, or piston, slid inside another tube. The piston was pulled back to let water flow into the tube. Then the piston was pushed in. It shot the water out the other end like a backyard "Supersoaker."

SPINOFFS

Irrigated fields need to be **fertilized** because the water washes away the nutrients in the soil, which plants need to grow. For thousands of years, poo (called "night soil" by the more delicate) was dumped on fields to do the job. The problem, though, was that this often spreads disease. So later chemists developed poo-free fertilizers.

The use of **wheels** to get water spun off another bright idea: Using wheels to get **power** from water!

The chain pump gave rise to another great invention: the **chain drive**. It combines a wheel and chain to transmit power. Think of the gears and chain on a bicycle.

The force pump inspired still another really important invention—the **internal combustion engine.**

Hey, Progress! Want a Drink?

Large-scale farming is just the start of what water pumps made possible in Mesopotamia. The settlements there spawned big deals like cities, trade, architecture, writing, and government.

Inventions: Water Screw, Archimedes Claw, Block and Tackle, and more

Archimedes

No one really knows for sure if Archimedes ran naked down the street shouting, "Eureka!" upon making a scientific discovery. But if it's true, it highlights one of the most interesting things about him: that he tended to become deeply absorbed in intellectual problems. So much so, that he could completely forget about the world around him. Some historians claim he became so engrossed by his thoughts, he would even forget to eat or wash!

It Was a Piece of *Pi*

Very little is known about Archimedes' life. He was born around 287 BCE in the Greek colony of Syracuse. He went to Alexandria, in Egypt, then the intellectual center of the world, to study. There, he met some of the greatest thinkers of the day.

Archimedes' main interest was mathematics, and it was in this field that he achieved his greatest successes. He figured out the value of *pi* in order to determine the circumference of a circle. He also worked out how to calculate the area of a circle, the volume of a sphere, and discovered the relationship between the volume of a sphere and a cylinder.

While in Alexandria, Archimedes began working as an engineer. This is most likely when he invented his water screw, which was probably used to empty water from the hold of one of King Hieron's ships.

The Crown Jewel of Science

The king gave Archimedes another royal problem to solve. He had arranged to have a jeweler make him a crown of gold, but suspected that the jeweler might have stolen some of the gold and substituted another metal. Archimedes' mission was to find out what the crown was actually made of.

According to the famous legend, Archimedes was taking a bath when he realized that the water level rose when he got in, and sank when he got out. From this observation, he determined that an object displaces water based on its density. Realizing he now had a way to measure the amount of gold in the crown, he jumped from the tub and ran through the streets shouting, "Eureka! I've found it!"

Archimedes solved the king's problem (the crown was actually a fake!). But even more importantly, he had discovered the scientific principle of specific gravity. Today, his breakthrough is known as Archimedes' Principle.

The Uplifting Power of Math

Many of Archimedes' inventions were developed while he was trying to prove his mathematical ideas. When he came up with a new theory, he would conduct an experiment to see if it was correct. One experiment resulted in an ingenious, new type of crane. By using a combination of levers and pulleys, he was able to move a heavy ship all by himself! Archimedes' reliance on logic, trial and error, and step-by-step experimentation led many to call him the Father of Experimental Science.

This Means War!

During the Second Punic War (218–201 BCE), Archimedes used his practical skills to help defend Syracuse from the Romans. He designed and built massive, rock-firing catapults and giant grappling hooks that could grasp a ship and dump it over. Another invention attributed to Archimedes may only be a myth, but it sounds impressive. It was a series of lenses and mirrors that focused the sun's rays onto the Roman ships. The "death ray" caused the ships to burst into flame!

Nitwit messengers! By the time your important message reaches its destination, "I need thirty-three packs of thread" has turned into "I kneaded thirteen sacks of bread." If only there were a way to record information so it wouldn't get mixed up or forgotten!

ALPHABET

By 3500 BCE, Mesopotamians were using a simple form of writing to record important information. It was called cuneiform (kew-NAY-i-form). A sharp stick called a stylus was used to scratch V-shapes into wet clay. There were more than twelve hundred different shapes. They represented objects, names, and numbers. When the clay dried, the scratches left a permanent written record.

Learning all of the symbols was not easy. Special schools sprang up to teach the symbols to would-be scribes. These were the first real schools anywhere in the world.

HIGHLIGHTS   Invented by: Still a mystery, possibly Canaanites (people fro

The word "alphabet" comes from the two first letters of the Greek alphabet, alpha and beta.

One of the earliest forms of writing was Egyptian **hieroglyphics**. It used pictures to represent words.

The Chinese developed their own form of writing by 1600 BCE.

That Sounds Great

Around 2600 BCE, the Sumerians had a sound idea. Instead of using thousands of symbols to represent the meanings of words, why not use just a few symbols to represent the sounds of words? The first phonographic (from the Greek words meaning "sound picture") alphabet was born.

The World's Best Graffiti

About 1800 BCE, mysterious foreigners living in Egypt— possibly Canaanites, a tribe related to the Hebrews—left an inscription on a stony cliff. Some researchers consider this the first true alphabet. It had only twenty-two letters, much fewer than any other writing system of the time. Plus, each of the letters represented only a single consonant sound—a big change. Each Egyptian hieroglyph, for example, could stand for several different sounds, or even whole, unrelated words!

I'd Like to Buy a Vowel

The new alphabet was much easier to learn and use than any previous writing system. The only problem with it was that it did not have any vowels. Did the letters "HT," for example, mean hit, hat, hate, or hot?

The next step then was to invent a way to represent vowel sounds in written language. The North Semites, Phoenicians, Ugarites, and ancient Hebrews all spelled out ways to do this between 1700 and 1000 BCE. These first true alphabets inspired many other languages, especially Greek, Arabic, Latin, and Cyrillic—the foundations of all the major languages of Europe!

Was it Important? You Alphabet Your Life it Was!

The alphabet gave everybody the chance to become literate, not just rich or educated people. This helped spread information around the world, and spurred the development of trade and innovation. It also made it possible for more people to create art like poetry, fiction, and drama, and to preserve their history and culture.

19

 AT SCHOOL

The first real school anywhere in the world was in Mesopotamia. It was formed to teach scribes how to write cuneiform symbols. Modern classrooms use inventions from all over the world.

Students used to use hand-held wooden slates painted with a mixture of egg white and burnt potato ash to do their work. **Chalk**, a powdery material made from the squished skeletons of tiny sea creatures, was used for writing.

Rubber comes from the sap of a South American tree. It got its name soon after Europeans discovered that lumps of the stuff could be used to "rub out" pencil marks.

The first-known **chairs** date from about 2600 BCE. They were found in the tombs of Egyptian pharaohs.

During the thirteenth century, King Edward I of England realized that using a person's arm as a measuring device was a problem. He ordered a measuring stick of iron be made to serve as the standard **ruler** for the entire kingdom. This stick was called the iron ulna. It got its name from the ulna, the bone in your forearm!

The first writing **ink** was invented in China, while credit for the first **pens** goes to the Romans.

The earliest versions of **scissors** were probably made in Egypt around 1500 BCE. They were constructed from a single piece of bronze bent into a U-shape.

British mathematician John Venn invented the—wait for it—**Venn diagram** in 1880.

Crayons were invented in 1903 in the United States by adding colors to paraffin wax to create a safe, easy-to-use drawing material.

After sailing with a Portuguese explorer to West Africa in 1486, German mapmaker and merchant Martin Behaim constructed the world's first **globe**. He called it Erdapfel—German for "Earth apple."

The **pencil** was invented more than four hundred years ago by a Swiss-German naturalist. Before that, people wrote with sticks of graphite (a flaky form of carbon) wrapped in string.

21

Producing thread is "sew" hard! Ha ha. Seriously, you need help.

SPINNING WHEEL

Early makers of clothing used things like leather strips, animal hair, or plant fibers as thread. People quickly learned you could make stronger thread if you twisted several fibers together.

About ten thousand years ago, women began using a simple tool called a drop spindle to do the twisting. It was basically a stick with a weight attached to it. The fibers would be wrapped around the stick. Then the spindle was dropped. Gravity would wind the fibers together (imagine a twisting yo-yo string).

The drop spindle was used for over nine thousand years to make thread for everything from mummy wrappings to tapestries, ropes, and sails. Unfortunately, using a drop spindle is hard work. It's slow, too.

I'm on Your Side

In the Middle Ages, a clever person somewhere in China, India, or Persia had the idea to turn a spindle on its side. She (it was probably a she, since women did most of the world's spinning) added a pulley and a drive wheel. This new and improved spindle was called a spinning wheel.

Using the spinning wheel, thread could be produced in half the time of the old method. Later, a foot pedal was added, which also let the spinners keep their hands free for other tasks.

By the thirteenth century, the spinning wheel had arrived in Europe, where clothing was always made at home. Making the thread was one of the hardest and most time-consuming parts of the job. With a spinning wheel, thread-making got a lot easier.

Easy-to-spin thread made producing fabric faster and cheaper. For the first time, it became practical to make cloth in a factory instead of at home.

SPINOFFS

In 1764, James Hargreaves invented a new-and-improved spinning wheel, called the **spinning jenny**. The jenny was several spinning wheels working together. It really cranked up the process of making yarn, used to make cloth.

Shortly after in 1768, an even better spinning machine was invented by Sir Richard Arkwright and John Kay. It was called a **water frame**. It was powered by—yup—moving water.

In 1771, Arkwright opened the very first **textile factory**. It was next to a river in Cromford Mill, England. One reason Arkwright chose Cromford for the factory was because there were lots of children there he could put to work!

Taking the World for a Spin

Combined with the loom—a machine that weaves the threads or yarns together to make cloth—the spinning wheel helped launch the Industrial Revolution. Textiles were the first industry to become "industrialized" in the 1700s.

You are HERE.
The stuff you want is THERE.
Wait, where's there again?

COMPASS

Traveling—and getting lost—has always been part of life. Ancient peoples used many tricks to keep on track. In daytime they used the sun as a guide. At night they followed the stars. They used landmarks to help them remember a route. They might even note the direction of migrating birds or of the wind to help guide them.

Water travel had even more challenges. Imagine getting caught in a storm on the open ocean, without any landmarks, birds, or stars to guide you. What would you do? That's easy—you'd panic!! Sailors sure did. So they didn't stray far from familiar places.

24

A Fortunate Discovery

Two thousand years ago, the Chinese discovered a mineral called a lodestone. It's magnetic, and always points in the same direction. Fortune tellers used the stones to help predict the future. To do so, they placed the lodestone on a board called a Luo Pan. The stone would spin, pointing to lucky dates for things like weddings or burials.

By about 83 CE, people figured that lodestones always pointed north-south. They could be used—duh!—to help you find your way while traveling. With that better-late-than-never realization, the first compass was born.

Floating Fish

Eventually, people realized the lodestone would rotate more easily if it were floating on water. The bobbing stones reminded observers of fish. These simple "floating fish" compasses were used by travelers for hundreds of years. Around 600 CE, the "fish"—er, I mean, stones—were replaced by magnetized needles.

Got it Covered

A Chinese sea captain discovered that needles float even better on oil than on water. But the oil made a mess when it sloshed onto the ship's decks! Another sailor solved the problem by putting the compass inside a glass-covered case. Finally, the magnetic compass was easy to use on land and at sea. By the end of the first century CE, Chinese sailors were using the compass to travel farther than any other ships in the world.

Did You Think of That Yourself?

Magnetic compasses appeared in Europe around 1100 CE. No one knows for sure if they were invented there, or if news of the invention was brought to Europe with traders from the East. One reason some historians think it was an independent invention is that European compasses always point north. Chinese compasses, however, have always pointed south.

SPINOFFS

In the 1600s, no one knew how compasses worked. Then William Gilbert, an English physician, suggested it was because Earth is a magnet! He was right.

In 1820, a Danish professor named Hans Christian Oersted hosted a demonstration of magnetism using a compass. He turned on an electric current to heat a wire. Whoa—the compass needle moved! He had no idea why. Oersted published his findings, hoping other scientists might solve the mystery. French scientist André-Marie Ampère did just that. He discovered that an electric current produces a magnetic field.

Michael Faraday, an English chemist, reasoned that if Ampère was correct, then a magnetic field could produce an electric current. Bingo! His discovery, the Principle of Induction, was unveiled in 1831.

Bravely Pointing the Way Forward

Now people could travel farther from home without getting lost. Explorers set out to discover new people and new lands.

So much information to record. You could sure use a light, long-lasting material to write it on...

PAPER

Throughout history, people tried to write on all kinds of materials:

In Mesopotamia, people etched letters into wet tablets of clay; in Egypt, people used papyrus, a paper-like material made from a marsh reed; in India, people wrote on palm leaves; in Europe, people inscribed wax tablets or parchment made from animal skins; in China, people inked info onto tortoise shells, bone, strips of bamboo, or silk cloth.

All of this stuff had drawbacks. Some, like stone, wood, or clay, were heavy and hard to move around. Others, like wax tablets or palm leaves, wouldn't last. Papyrus only grows in North tropical Africa. And silk was—ka-ching!—far too pricey.

HIGHLIGHTS   Invented by: Cai Lun   When: 105 CE   Where: China

Keep a Record

Since about 300 CE, a paper-like material was made in China from mulberry and hemp fibers. The fibers were beaten to a pulp, then spread out to dry. This paper was too rough and knobbly to be used for writing. Instead, it was used for clothing!

Cai Lun, a record keeper for the Chinese Imperial court during the Han Dynasty (206 BCE–220 CE), had probably seen this paper. Cai Lun's job meant that he would write down his information on bamboo strips or squares of silk. He didn't like using either one, though, so Cai Lun began to look for other materials.

With the help of Deng Sui (who later became Empress), Cai Lun set about improving the thick paper. He mixed different amounts of tree bark, fishnets, and bamboo with water, then rolled the soupy mash onto a fine screen to dry. His sheets of paper turned out thin, light, smooth, and useful for writing.

In China, Cai Lun became a hero. His invention was considered so important that the government kept the method secret for more than six hundred years!

In 751 CE, some Chinese papermakers were captured during a battle. Their captors learned the secrets of papermaking. Traders then spread the know-how to the rest of the world.

Note to Self: Paper Rules!

It's pretty easy to take paper for granted but it changed how people communicated and stored information. Paper helped ideas spread and made it more likely for people to build on those innovations with even bigger ideas of their own.

"Wood" It Work?

Around 1000 CE, Europeans began to make their own paper from rags. Then one day in 1719, French naturalist René de Reaumur saw a wasp chewing on wood, then spitting out the mush to form its nest. Reaumur saw that the wasp's nest resembled paper—could he learn the secret of how to make paper from the wasps?

Reaumur succeeded. Paper made from wood pulp was born. About one hundred and twenty years later, the Canadian inventor Charles Fenerty built upon Reaumur's discovery. He invented the process of papermaking we still use today.

IN THE BATHROOM

Bathrooms first appeared in the Indus Valley (in modern Pakistan and India) about four thousand years ago. Check out these fun facts about some of the most common inventions you'll find in the modern lavatory.

The first archeological evidence of **makeup** is from ancient Egypt. Kohl was an eye makeup used by Egyptian queens. The Egyptians also used eye shadow made from a green mineral called malachite and a lipstick made from clay called red ochre.

The first **mirrors** appeared around five thousand years ago. They were made from highly polished bronze or copper disks. Glass-backed mirrors, like the ones used today, were invented in Venice, Italy, around the year 1300.

Legend has it that terry-cloth **towels** (like what we use today) were invented in Bursa, Turkey.

Credit for inventing **soap** for washing the body goes to the Phoenicians in about 600 BCE. The soap was a mixture of melted goat fat, or tallow, and ashes.

Floss was invented by a dentist in 1815, who recommended using strands of silk.

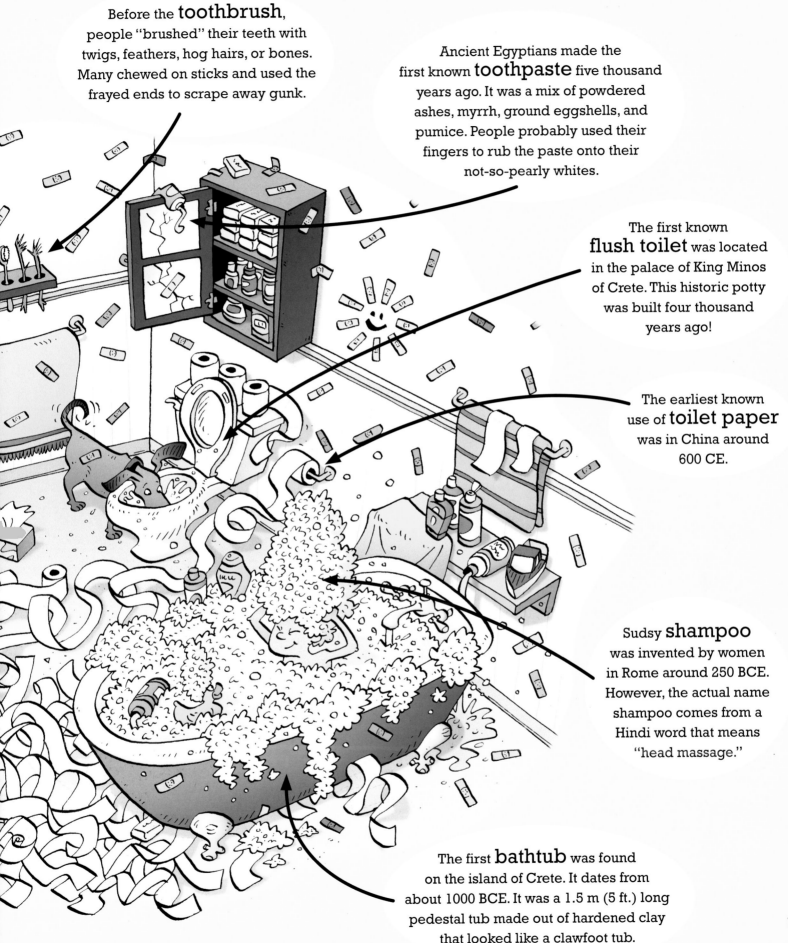

Before the **toothbrush**, people "brushed" their teeth with twigs, feathers, hog hairs, or bones. Many chewed on sticks and used the frayed ends to scrape away gunk.

Ancient Egyptians made the first known **toothpaste** five thousand years ago. It was a mix of powdered ashes, myrrh, ground eggshells, and pumice. People probably used their fingers to rub the paste onto their not-so-pearly whites.

The first known **flush toilet** was located in the palace of King Minos of Crete. This historic potty was built four thousand years ago!

The earliest known use of **toilet paper** was in China around 600 CE.

Sudsy **shampoo** was invented by women in Rome around 250 BCE. However, the actual name shampoo comes from a Hindi word that means "head massage."

The first **bathtub** was found on the island of Crete. It dates from about 1000 BCE. It was a 1.5 m (5 ft.) long pedestal tub made out of hardened clay that looked like a clawfoot tub.

Long Ago....

From Handmade to Factory Made

The switch-over to farming was a major turning point in history. After that, things settled down for a while. That's not to say that nothing new was invented—it's just that little changed from year to year or generation to generation. People lived in small communities and never traveled far from where they were born.

Nevertheless, thousands of inventions slowly accumulated over time, each one spinning off dozens of other innovations. By the middle of the eighteenth century, the pace and quality of inventions had become so great that they would usher in a second major turning point: The Industrial Revolution.

During this time (approximately 1750–1900), previously homemade goods, such as cloth, began to be manufactured in factories. New materials, such as steel, made products both stronger and cheaper. Technologies, such as steam power and electricity, made travel easier, people more productive (since you could now work after dark), and food more available to all.

Like most big changes, there were also down sides—the biggest being increased pollution from factories that choked the air with smog. But this revolution was about more than just products. For the first time, workers began to join together and fight for their rights. This led to societies where average people had a greater say in things like government than ever before.

You've been copying the text of a book all day to make a new one. Your hand hurts, but hey, you're on page six—only three hundred pages to go! Oh, boy...

PRINTING PRESS

Many ancient civilizations had different forms of "books." In Mesopotamia, they were made from carved clay tablets. In China, bamboo strips were inscribed with text and tied together with string. European books were written with pen and ink on vellum or parchment. In South America, the Maya made folded books from tree bark. These books all had the same drawback—each one had to be copied by hand. It was slow work. Plus, it was all too easy to make ~~coping copyng~~ copying mistakes.

HIGHLIGHTS   Invented by: Johann Gutenberg   When: 1455   Where

No Stone Unturned

Around 400 CE, Chinese artists began cutting designs into the surface of a flat stone. They spread ink over the artwork, and then transferred the design to a sheet of paper by pressing it against the wet stone. This style of printing, called lithography (from Greek words meaning stone and writing), is still used by artists today.

Scribes adapted the artists' technique by chiseling the text of entire documents into a single wooden block. The method sped up the copying process, but still had its issues. For example, if you made even a tiny carving mistake, the entire block was ruined!

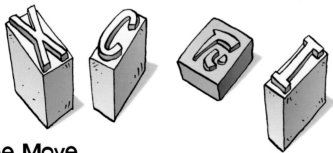

On The Move

In about 1045, a printer named Bi Sheng came up with an impressive improvement. It was called movable type. Instead of carving one large block, he created an entire set of individual characters from clay. He stuck the ones he needed into a tray filled with hot wax. When the wax cooled, the letters were fixed in place. Bi Sheng could then print his text as many times as he wished. When he wanted to change his text, all he had to do was melt the wax and reset the letters.

Gutenberg Turns a New Leaf

It was 1438. Back in Europe, many people were trying to come up with their own way to replace hand copying. Johann Gutenberg was a goldsmith, and brought knowledge of metal and fine workmanship to the task.

Gutenberg's breakthrough came from two original ideas. First, instead of using a roller to apply the ink, Gutenberg used a modified olive or wine-making press. Secondly, he came up with a better way to make metal movable type. It was called typecasting. He produced the first printed book, a Bible, in 1455.

By 1480, there were printing presses in more than one hundred European towns. By 1500, that number had almost tripled. The presses produced more than thirty thousand books—totaling twenty million copies in all—in that same year.

It Really Spread the Word!

The printing press helped spread information faster, farther, and to more people than ever before. And since it was easier to make books, they were cheaper, too. More affordable books meant that more people could also learn to read. That's one smart invention!

BIGTHINKERS

Inventions: Self-propelled car, diving bell, bicycle, helicopter, parachute, drilling machine, siege ladder, automatic bobbin winder, lens grinding machine, submarine, and hundreds more!

Leonardo da Vinci

Leonardo da Vinci was the world's original Renaissance Man—someone who is interested in many different areas, and is good at them all! Da Vinci was a world-famous artist, scientist, architect, and the inventor of incredible machines that were far ahead of his time.

Da Vinci was born in Italy in 1452. Even as a child, he was gifted in many areas, including drawing and music. A few of his early sketches showed how different machine parts worked.

At fourteen, he became an apprentice to Italy's leading painter and sculptor, Andrea de Verrocchio. In de Verrocchio's studio, da Vinci learned all the skills of an artist. He also studied subjects as varied as metalworking, chemistry, mechanics, anatomy, and carpentry!

Da Vinci kept detailed notebooks his whole life, which he wrote in nearly every day. Using a backward script that could only be read using a mirror, he routinely jotted down all kinds of observations, ideas, sketches, and calculations. No one knows for sure why he wrote backward. Some think that it was because da Vinci was left-handed. Others think he may have wanted to keep his ideas secret.

Da Vinci finds inspiration...

Duking It Out

In 1482, da Vinci approached the Duke of Milan, one of the most powerful men in Italy. Leonardo had an astonishing proposal: Even though he had no practical experience outside of the art studio, he wanted the duke to hire him to design large-scale projects—everything from bridges to ships! The duke agreed. Da Vinci was named the engineer of Milan and worked for the duke for seventeen years.

The duke kept him busy with construction jobs, painting, and sculpting. Da Vinci also worked on his own investigations, including studies of nature, clocks, canals, and fortresses. He also discovered significant insights into how blood circulates in the body, how the moon affects tides, and even how the eye works.

Thanks to his broad knowledge, da Vinci was able to see patterns and relationships where few others could. When he studied muscles and bones, he saw how similar they were to levers and gears. When he examined how water moves, he noticed that air moves in the same ways.

Da Vinci's only problem, it seems, was that he couldn't stick to any one subject. He often didn't finish the projects he started!

Thinking It Through

For da Vinci, it wasn't enough to be told the reason for something—he wanted to see it with his own eyes. In his journals, he once wrote, "In dealing with a scientific problem, I first arrange several experiments, and then show with reasons why such an experiment must necessarily operate in this and in no other way."

In 1502, he went to work for Cesare Borgia, another rich and powerful duke. He worked as the duke's chief architect and engineer.

It was during this period that da Vinci painted his most famous portrait, the *Mona Lisa*. People have been fascinated by her mysterious smile ever since. Its appeal may lie in a trick da Vinci learned from studying the human eye. He discovered that shadows seem to disappear when you look right at them. They reappear if you glimpse them from the corner of your eye. Da Vinci painted the haunting smile using nothing but shadows!

In 1516, da Vinci entered the service of King Francis I of France. He lived at the King's chateau in France until his death in 1519. It is said that the King himself was holding him in his arms when da Vinci died.

Hey! See that tiny little bug that's about to bite yo—oops. Too late.
Okay, see that ship that's about to attack yo—oops. Too late.
You know what you could really use...?

LENSES

Water was likely the first way that people magnified objects. They might have noticed how a drop of water on a leaf made it easier to see the leaf's veins underneath it. This is because the curved drop acts like a magnifier. As early as the fifth century BCE in Greece, people used droplets like these to get a closer look at their work.

Using water as a magnifier has drawbacks. First of all, it makes things wet. Secondly, water drops don't just sit there—they tend to drip or dry up. Curved bits of rock crystals or glass, called lenses, make better magnifiers. They don't evaporate or leave splotches.

HIGHLIGHTS Invented by: Hans Lippershey, Hans & Zacharias Janssen, or Jac

Spectacular Spectacles

It wasn't until after 1450 that lenses were used in a truly practical way: as eyeglasses. At first, spectacles were only worn by the very rich or highly educated. But when the printing press was invented in 1455, reading became more popular. The demand for glasses boomed, making fashion eyewear a big business, especially in the Netherlands.

Real Visionaries

Around 1600, a Dutch lens-maker discovered that if you peer through two lenses at the same time, they magnify better than a single lens. Who was this eagle-eyed visionary? The answer is anything if clear, but rival claims have been put forward for at least three different inventors: Hans Lippershey, Hans Janssen and his son Zacharias, and Jacob (or James) Metius. The most likely story is that since more people than ever were experimenting with lenses, several people came up with the same idea at about the same time.

Eye Spy Stories

There are just as many stories for how the "spyglass," or telescope, was invented, too. One story goes that as one of the Janssens was polishing a spectacle lens, he held it up to examine it. He decided to check it in more detail by looking at it through another lens. To his utter amazement, the clock on a distant church tower suddenly seemed close enough to touch! A very similar story is told about Lippershey, his assistant, and a church steeple.

The Story of the Microscope

While many people were interested in using the telescope to make faraway images seem closer, others wanted to make tiny objects seem larger. Like the telescope, no one is sure who made the first microscope. The Janssens, however, were manufacturing microscopes as early as 1595. Although the earliest microscopes weren't very powerful, they opened up a fascinating miniature world in greater detail than was ever possible before. Now people could study creepy crawly critters with the popular "flea glasses."

SPINOFFS

Italian inventor Galileo Galilei learned about the Dutch "looker," or telescope. He built his own version in 1609. Galileo was the first to see the surface of the moon. He also drew the first map of the largest stars in the Milky Way.

Around 1665, British scientist Robert Hooke began examining slices of cork under his microscope. He saw that the tissue was made up of repeating shapes. He called the shapes cells. He had discovered the building blocks of all living things.

In 1673, Dutch scientist Antoni van Leeuwenhoek wrote about a brand new universe he found—in water! He detailed all kinds of swimming microscopic creatures, including parasites and bacteria.

Hey, This Looks Important!

Clearly! Using lenses in telescopes improved ship navigation, which helped people find new places to explore and trade their goods. The microscope let scientists see all kinds of teensy germs and bacteria, which led to improvements in people's health.

You're late for school. Again! How is anyone supposed to be on time if no one knows what time it is in the first place? If only you had an...

ACCURATE CLOCK

In olden days, people could keep track of time by watching the sun move across the sky. In olden nights, they could clock the movements of the moon and stars. Sort of. Neither method was very accurate. Around 1400 BCE, the Egyptians came up with a new way to measure time. It was as exciting as watching water drip—in fact, it *was* watching water drip! Time was told by the amount of water that dripped out of a bucket-shaped container.

38

HIGHLIGHTS Invented by: Christiaan Huygens   When: 1656–1657   Wher

Drip, Drip, Drip

Around 325 BCE, the Greeks began using these water clocks, too. They called them clepsydras, which means "water thief." The clocks didn't work very well because it was hard to keep the water flowing through them in a steady stream. When the flow of water slowed to a dribble, so did the clock.

A Shadowy Past is Left Behind

Sundials were the most popular form of timekeeping device in Europe until the Middle Ages. Then, around 1275 CE, new kinds of clocks appeared. They were big and heavy, and were operated using a geared, weight-driven mechanical device called an escapement.

What made the times right for this clunky clock? First of all, towns were bustling with new opportunities in business and trade, and merchants needed to operate on a schedule to make money. Another reason was that both the Christian and Muslim faiths required people to pray at regular times of day. Weight-driven clocks were often placed at the top of tall church towers so that everyone in town could see them. While these clocks were better than earlier versions, they still did not keep accurate time. Most didn't even have minute hands!

Spring Time

Another kind of clock, invented around 1430, was powered by a spring. The spring-powered clocks could be much smaller than weight-driven clocks. So much smaller, in fact, that in 1500 a German locksmith named Peter Henlein made tiny, portable, spring-driven clocks that he nicknamed "Nuremberg eggs." Cute.

Swing Time

In 1656, Dutch scientist Christiaan Huygens had a timely idea. Building on an idea of Italian inventor Galileo Galilei's—that clocks could be driven by swinging pendulums—Huygens set to work. The first pendulum clock he built was the most accurate clock yet. Then Huygens began tinkering with Henlein's eggs. His improvements made the spring-driven clock much more accurate, too. Minute hands could even be added. In addition, the clocks were portable. Suddenly, pocket and wristwatches could be made. Now what's your excuse for being late?

SPINOFFS

Pendulum clocks were the first accurate clocks. Since then, quartz, digital, and atomic clocks have been developed, which keep time even better.

As transportation improved, it became more important that different towns operate on a standard time schedule. In 1884, the world officially adopted Canadian railway planner and engineer Sir Sanford Fleming's plan for establishing different time zones.

Early calculators used clockwork mechanisms in them, and were even called "calculating clocks"!

It Keeps You on Time!

Staying in sync with everyone else made meeting for business (or pleasure) a breeze. Smaller, more accurate clocks also made for smoother sailing—because sailors relied on measuring elapsed time to determine their longitude (how far east or west they were) at sea.

You own a mine and business is booming—except that the deeper you dig, more water floods into your mine. You need a machine with the power to pump out all that unwanted water. You need a...

STEAM ENGINE

In 300 BCE, a Greek named Hero invented an incredible device that used steam to open the doors of a temple. It worked like this: A fire was lit on the temple's altar. The fire heated a container of water. When the water boiled, steam rose from it and flowed into a series of pipes. The pipes directed the steam to the temple doors. As the steam flowed out, it pushed the doors open!

This is the first written record of steam being used as a power source.

Where Are My Glasses?

Jump ahead two thousand years to the late 1600s. Glassmakers in Great Britain needed tons of coal to keep the furnaces that melted their raw materials blazing. Coal came from mines. The mines were constantly flooding, which slowed coal production to a mere dribble. Big bucks could be made by anyone who could come up with a cheap method to keep the mines drained and the coal coming.

In 1698, a military engineer named Thomas Savery came up with an idea for a new kind of pump. Like Hero's invention, it used steam as its power source. Savery's pump became known as the "Miner's Friend." Unfortunately, it was more a fiend than a friend. It had a bad habit of blowing up.

A Newcomen on the Scene

In 1712, English blacksmith Thomas Newcomen invented his own steam-powered pump. It used atmospheric pressure to help it work. Newcomen's pump had two main advantages over Savery's: It was reliable and easy to maintain. On the downside, the pumps wasted a lot of energy.

From Steam Pump to Steam Engine

Between 1765 and 1769, Scottish engineer James Watt was called to repair a few broken Newcomen pumps. He realized a few changes would make the machine far easier and efficient to operate.

He rolled up his sleeves and went to work. First, he closed off one part of the pump. Then, he added a "steam jacket" that insulated it so it would stay hot. Finally, he invented a separate steam condenser chamber so that water could be recirculated and used again. These changes made Watt's engine five times more efficient than the Newcomen model and seventy-five percent less expensive to use!

Watt's steam engine made mining easier, safer, and less expensive. Coal, iron, and other raw materials could now be obtained at better prices and in larger quantities. Other industries also benefited from the steam engine, like textile mills.

How the Steam Engine Works

1. Fuel is burned in a firebox.
2. It boils water in the boiler, producing steam.
3. The steam is transferred to the motor unit via the heat exchange.
4. The motor unit turns the heat energy into mechanical energy. This is just a fancy way of saying it turns the heat into physical force. Now the engine has power to pull a train, pump water, or whatever else you need.

It Was More Than Just Hot Air!

The steam engine got the Industrial Revolution off the ground in two ways. First, it made it easier to get the raw materials from mines and it powered factories. Later on, it revolutionized transportation by powering both the railroad, in 1804, and the steamship, in 1807. Go steam!

Man, steel sure is useful stuff.
So strong! So flexible!
So...difficult to make.
If only we could figure out
how to make it more easily...

STEEL

The first weapons were sticks and stones. Then people discovered metals like gold and silver, but these were too soft for weapon-making, so they were mostly used for jewelry and decorations. Next, people discovered that by melting down two soft metals and mixing them together, they could create a stronger metal, called an alloy. Copper and tin were mixed together and made bronze, which could be used to make swords and knives. Around 2000 BCE, improvements to kilns and furnaces (where metals were melted) meant people could make iron, a metal that needs a higher temperature to melt, but is stronger than bronze.

HIGHLIGHTS Invented by: Henry Bessemer   When: 1855   Where: Gre

What is Steel?

Steel is a form of iron that is both stronger and more flexible than the ordinary stuff. The secret ingredient in making steel is carbon. Too little carbon mixed with iron makes metal that is too flexible (wrought iron). Too much carbon makes a metal that is hard, but brittle (cast iron). Adding just the right amount of carbon gives you flexible, meltable steel. But people didn't learn this until thousands of years after the first steel was made. Without that knowledge, making steel consistently was tricky.

Steel Works

During the second century BCE, the Chinese figured out a way to make steel in a super-hot furnace called a blast furnace. They "blasted" oxygen into the furnace to remove some of the carbon in cast iron. They called their process the "hundred refinings method" since it had to be repeated more than one hundred times before it worked!

The Chinese used steel mostly for making weapons. It was strong and could hold a sharp edge better than other metals. And, since their weapons were so much better than their neighbors', the Chinese were able to dominate nearby territories for hundreds of years!

The Million Dollar Question

Methods of making steel were being used around the world by the seventeenth century, but it was expensive and difficult to make the metal. The challenge was how to make steel efficiently and cheaply. In 1855, a British inventor named Henry Bessemer invented a mechanism called a converter that could do just that. The Bessemer converter also blew air through the molten, or melted, iron, but allowed for huge amounts of steel to be made at once. The effect was immediate and huge! Cheap steel provided the backbone for dozens of industries.

Steel Stole Our Hearts!

Cheap steel is, literally, the foundation for modern industry. Suddenly, the metal was no longer only useful for a few select weapons. Buildings, bridges, tunnels, tools, machinery, airplanes, trains, ships, cars, and so much more—they are all made using steel.

What if you could generate power wherever you needed it, whenever you needed it? Sounds like a job for the...

ELECTRIC BATTERY

People knew about electricity thousands of years ago.

Lightning and electric eels that gave stunning shocks were both well known. However, no one really understood how to control electricity or use it for power.

44

HIGHLIGHTS Invented by: Alessandro Volta   When: 1800   Where: Italy

The Shocking Secret: Found—Then Lost!

Incredibly, the secret of generating electricity from chemicals was known in ancient times. Archeologists discovered a sophisticated battery in an ancient tomb near Baghdad. It was made from a clay jar. When filled with vinegar, the jar-battery would have been able to generate 1.1 volts of electricity. Unfortunately, the ancient batteries disappeared from use. The secret of making them was lost for almost two thousand years!

Nothing but Static

The next attempts at generating electricity weren't until the seventeenth century. German engineer Otto von Guericke built a device that held a glob of sulfur in a glass ball. When the ball was rubbed, electricity collected, much like when you rub a balloon against a sweater. Feathers and bits of paper would stick to the ball, and if you touched it with your finger, you'd get a little shock! Von Guericke didn't know it, but he was experimenting with static electricity.

Great Hoppin' Frog's Legs!

In 1780, Italian scientist Luigi Galvani began experimenting with frogs' legs. He wondered why they twitched when they were touched with a scalpel, even after the frog was dead. Was electricity at work? And if so, what was the source? Galvani suggested the electricity was coming from fluids in the frog's body.

Battery Up!

Another Italian scientist named Alessandro Volta thought Galvani was mistaken. He believed electrical activity was generated when the frog was touched by two different types of metal, such as iron and brass. Volta set to work to see if his theory was right. In 1800, he piled up alternating disks of two metals, this time copper and zinc. Then he bathed them in salt water—a less gruesome version of frog juice. His contraption, called a voltaic pile, worked. It generated a flow of electricity from one end of the pile to the other.

SPARKPLUGS

In 1745, Pieter van Musschenbroek invented the Leyden jar to store energy for later use. It became the basis for the capacitor, a device used in radios, TVs, computers, and camera flashes.

Benjamin Franklin did his kite experiment while investigating a way to prevent gunpowder stores from catching fire during lightning storms. With the knowledge he gathered, Franklin invented the lightning rod. This device protects tall buildings from lightning by carrying electricity away from the building and safely into the ground.

Pile On!

The voltaic pile was the first device that could convert chemical energy to electrical energy. Today, his invention is known as a dry cell. When dry cells are hooked together in a chain, they're called batteries. Scientists were able to do more and better experiments that used electricity. As a result, the pace of research picked up. Incredible new inventions and discoveries were just around the corner.

It Charged Our Lives!

The battery allowed electricity to be reliably generated in a steady stream—it was even portable! This ushered in a new age of electrical experiments and devices that eventually led to stuff like light bulbs, TVs, fridges, cars, and computers. Zap!

Ick—this apple has gone mushy. Yuck—that ham's gone slimy and smells like an old sneaker! If only there was a way to keep food fresh and safe for a long time!

FOOD CANNING

Many ingenious methods have been invented to preserve food. For instance, salting food prevents bacteria from growing in it. Adding tons of sugar, as in jams and preserves, also keeps foods from spoiling. Drying food can make it last for years. So can pickling, smoking, curing, and freezing it. None of these methods is perfect. They change the flavor and texture of foods. They are also difficult to do well, and if not prepared properly, the foods can spoil.

46

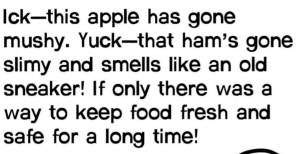

A Very Long Lunch Break

Throughout history, keeping soldiers fed was a constant problem. Not only did the troops need huge amounts of food, but the food had to be transported long distances to the front lines. During the winter, there wasn't any food at all to feed the soldiers. They all went home. War had to wait for the next fall—when summer's harvests were in.

Wine Not?

In the late 1700s, French general (later Emperor) Napoleon Bonaparte's huge army was spread across Europe and was running out of food. France offered a reward to the first person who could come up with a cheap method for preserving food for their troops. French candymaker Nicolas Appert had noticed that wine kept in glass bottles lasted indefinitely. He thought, "If it works for wine, why not for food?" He experimented for about a decade. His best results came from cooking food in glass jars and sealing them while still hot. Appert was awarded the cash prize, but unfortunately for Napoleon, French transportation was so lousy the food didn't reach the army until after the war ended!

Can It!

There were two big problems with Appert's method. Glass jars are heavy, and also tend to break. In 1810, Englishman Peter Durand experimented by bending sheets of tin into cylinders to make canisters. Food was cooked and sealed into the canisters at a factory. The new canisters, or cans for short, were unbreakable. They were cheaper and quicker to make than glass jars, too.

A Ghostly Invention

In 1873, American Amanda Theodosia Jones figured out how to can fresh, *uncooked* food. It involved removing the air from the can before it was sealed—this is called vacuum sealing. It was safer and tastier than earlier canned goods. Strangely, Jones claimed she had received instructions for her invention from ghostly spirits!

SPINOFFS

Soldiers liked canned foods. The only problem was opening the cans. They had to be cut open with bayonets, or smashed with rocks! The first functional **can opener** wasn't invented until almost fifty years later!

Half a century after canning was invented, French scientist Louis Pasteur discovered how it prevented food from spoiling: The heating process killed any germs in the food, and the seal kept new bacteria out. He would later create a process to prevent milk from spoiling known as **pasteurization**.

Its Influence Is Sealed!

By the 1900s, canned foods had become an everyday part of life. Canned food was cheap and convenient. Since people didn't have to spend time every day shopping for or preparing fresh food, they could focus on other things, like having fun or, oh yeah, working.

When: Late 1700s and 1810   Where: France and Great Britain

AT WAR

Throughout history, warfare has triggered the development of more inventions than almost any other human activity. You'll have a blast uncovering the secrets behind these familiar products and tools.

Invented to help people escape from tall, burning buildings, **parachutes** spun off another lifesaving invention: the **disposable diaper!**

The **crossbow**, invented around 400 BCE in China, was also used to shoot cables across canyons to make bridges!

In 1774, John Wilkinson invented a **drilling machine** powered by a water wheel that could bore straight, even holes into metal cylinders. He used the machine to make the most accurate cannons ever designed. Wilkinson's technique changed how tools were made from then on.

In 1940, actress Hedy Lamarr and composer George Antheil invented **Code Division Multiple Access** (CDMA) for the U.S. Military. It's also the technology behind **cell phones**.

In 1821, a writing method using raised dots was developed so that French soldiers could read in the dark. By 1824, Louis **Braille**, who was blind, had developed a complete system based on this for finger reading.

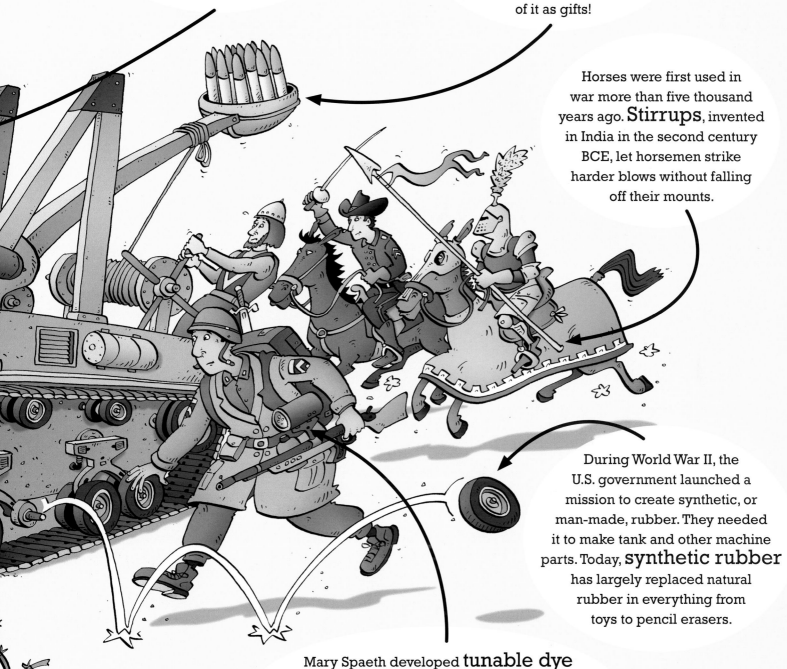

In 1869, Napoleon III of France offered a reward to anyone who came up with a cheap substitute for butter to feed his army. A chemist named Hippolyte Mège-Mouriés invented "oleomargarine"—a mixture of liquid beef fat, milk, water, and chopped cow's udder—the first **margarine**.

In Greece in the third century BCE, Archimedes designed a **catapult**. To add power, twisted hairs were used to hold back the catapult's arm. Hair became so valuable that Greek cities often gave each other piles of it as gifts!

Horses were first used in war more than five thousand years ago. **Stirrups**, invented in India in the second century BCE, let horsemen strike harder blows without falling off their mounts.

During World War II, the U.S. government launched a mission to create synthetic, or man-made, rubber. They needed it to make tank and other machine parts. Today, **synthetic rubber** has largely replaced natural rubber in everything from toys to pencil erasers.

Mary Spaeth developed **tunable dye lasers** for the U.S. Army in 1966. This technology let people adjust the exact frequency of a laser. It is now used in **barcode scanners** at supermarket checkouts.

Too bad no one believed you about those aliens in your front yard. If only you could have taken a...

PHOTOGRAPH

Way back in 350 BCE, Greek philosopher Aristotle described how a hole poked through a window shutter would allow light to create faint images on the opposite wall. In a pre-TV age, this device—the camera obscura—was considered grand fun.

In the eleventh century, Muslim scientist, astronomer, and mathematician Alhazan was the first to describe how a camera obscura worked after experimenting with lamps in a darkened room in Cairo, Egypt. His published work was translated into Latin and read by scientists in Europe.

By the nineteenth century, a tabletop camera obscura was a popular party trick. Artists and scientists, however, saw the potential for something more. They wanted to come up with a way to make the pictures permanent.

HIGHLIGHTS Invented by: Joseph Nicéphore Niépce   When: 1826   Wher

The First Picture

Around 1813, French inventor Joseph Nicéphore Niépce got interested in printing. He drew pictures onto metal that was coated with light-sensitive materials, then exposed them to sunlight. The results were heliographes, French for "sun-drawings." In 1826, he combined a camera obscura with his specially coated sheets of paper and took the world's first photograph—of a pigeon roost!

Not Your Average Diorama

In 1825, French theater designer Louis Daguerre heard about Niépce's work. Daguerre was already famous for creating awesome stage illusions using large-scale 3-D models called dioramas. He thought Niépce's process might shorten the time it took to make the dioramas.

Daguerre and Niépce met in 1827. Even though Niépce didn't want to give away his secret invention, he agreed to work with Daguerre because he was broke! When Niépce died suddenly in 1833, Daguerre kept experimenting. Eventually he came up with improvements to Niépce's process, which produced sharper images and took far less time to make. He called the results Daguerreotypes.

And—Roll 'Em!

By 1877 photography was hot! But camera gear was messy. Photographers had to carry lots of chemicals and heavy equipment wherever they went.

George Eastman, a keen American photographer, invented the dry-plate photographic process after photo chemicals spilled all over his suitcase. He also invented the first rolls of film, and an easy-to-carry camera that let ordinary people take pictures just about anywhere. He named the camera "Kodak." By 1900, Eastman's company was mass-producing "Brownie" cameras, selling them for as little as $1. So say cheese! Now anyone, anywhere, could take snapshots.

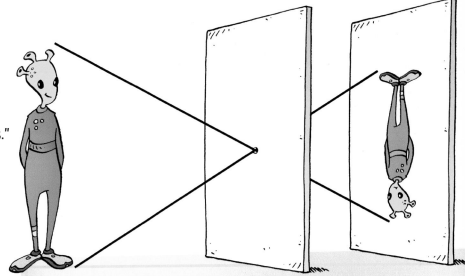

How a camera obscura works

1. Light hits an object, then bounces off it and travels through a tiny hole.
2. The light hits a darkened surface on the other side of the opening.
3. Woo hoo! The image of the object appears on the darkened surface, but smaller and upside down.

Want to turn this camera obscura into a real camera? Just add a lens to the hole, and a light sensitive material to capture the upside-down image. Poof! You've made yourself a photograph!

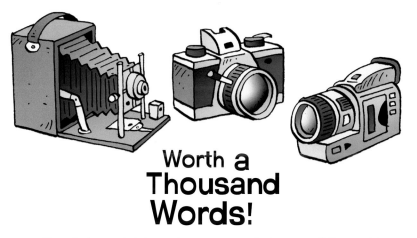

Worth a Thousand Words!

The photograph let people save accurate images of the world and events around them for the first time. This made it easier to share information, change people's ideas, and capture embarrassing images of friends and family for years to come.

You've used animal, water, and wind power to help you with your work. But you're still providing much of the power yourself to get your chores done. It's time to take charge with the...

ELECTRIC MOTOR

At the start of the eighteenth century, there was a frenzy of experiments involving electricity and magnetism. Benjamin Franklin comfirmed that lightning was a form of electricity. Alessandro Volta showed that electricity could be controlled to make a spark, and Hans Christian Oersted found that an electrical current could make a compass needle move!

HIGHLIGHTS   Invented by: Michael Faraday   When: 1821   Where: Gre

Faraday's Far-out Idea

British scientist Michael Faraday decided to build upon these experiments. He thought he could convert electrical energy into mechanical energy. If he was right, then electricity and magnets could be used to provide power and do work.

Spin-o-rama!

Faraday arranged a metal wire so that each end went into a cup of mercury. He then placed magnets at the bottom of each cup. In one cup, he attached the wire to the magnet so that the wire could not move, but the magnet could. In the second cup, the wire was able to move, but the magnet was fixed.

When Faraday applied an electric current to the wire, it flowed through the wire and produced an electric field. The free magnet started to spin. So did the loose end of the wire! From this experiment, Faraday had shown that electricity could be converted into motion. He had invented the world's first electric motor.

SPINOFFS

Michael Faraday believed that the forces of nature were connected. With this idea as his inspiration, he succeeded at creating a device that worked in the exact opposite way to the motor. By rotating a copper disk between the two poles of a horseshoe magnet, Faraday was able to generate an electric current. He had turned motion into energy! Faraday's device, called a Faraday disk, was the first **electromagnetic generator**. With it, all kinds of machinery could now be powered by electricity. Lights, factories, appliances, and any device that required energy could be operated without raising a sweat.

We Were Up and Running!

The electric motor really set things in motion. Motors operated the mills and factories of the Industrial Revolution. Even after almost two centuries of giant innovations, virtually all the machines and conveniences of modern life are powered by versions of Faraday's inventions.

Inventions: Electric motor and electric generator

Michael Faraday

Sometimes, no matter how hard you try, you can't solve a problem on your own. But people who know how to work with and learn from others can come up with far better ideas than they might on their own. Michael Faraday was one such person.

When he was twenty-three, Faraday approached the famous scientist Sir Humphry Davy for a job helping him in his lab. He got one! The job wasn't exactly what he expected. He was treated more like a lowly servant than a respectable lab assistant.

Once, when Davy went on a long trip to Europe, Faraday was asked to come along—as Davy's manservant. Davy's wife treated him terribly. She made him eat with the other servants and would not let him ride in the same coach as her and Davy. Faraday was so miserable on the trip, he even considered quitting science altogether!

But Faraday realized that he could learn a lot from Davy. Staying on good terms with one of the most brilliant scientists of the day was a priceless gift to such a curious, ambitious young man.

By traveling with Davy, Faraday also learned from other scientists and philosophers they met during the two-year journey. By the end of the trip, he was ready to start a career of his own.

Davy and Faraday at work in the lab.

Breaking Away

At the age of twenty-five, Faraday began his own scientific career as a chemist. His hard work and experience helped him to discover several new chemicals, but Faraday really wanted to work with electricity. Davy talked him out of it, suggesting he work with light and lenses instead. Faraday spent eight years working unsuccessfully on optics. Some researchers think Davy intentionally steered him away from the areas where he was likely to succeed, out of jealousy for Faraday's talent.

A Powerful Idea

In 1819, Hans Christian Oersted had discovered the existence of magnetic fields. This finding led to Alessandro Volta's invention of the electric battery. Faraday decided to follow up on these developments with his own research into electromagnetism.

Just two years later, he had a major breakthrough when he figured out how to make an electric motor. How did Faraday come up with his idea? By brainstorming with others. He had discussed the electric motor with Davy and

another scientist, William Hyde Wollaston. They had experimented with motors but could not come up with a design that worked. By learning from their mistakes, Faraday was able to succeed where they had failed.

Generating More Excitement

Still, Faraday always wanted to learn more. In 1831, he came up with another idea: electromagnetic induction. Like his earlier ideas, it drew upon knowledge collected by many people. This principle showed that you could not only turn electrical energy into mechanical energy, but you could make the opposite conversion too—turning mechanical energy into electricity! Faraday had invented the world's first electric generator.

His ideas stimulated other scientists to work on their own ideas. James Clerk Maxwell developed mathematical formulas based on Faraday's equations. Guglielmo Marconi used Maxwell's formulas to invent the first wireless communication device—the radio. Thomas Edison carried on Faraday's work and built the first power plant.

Hey there! I've got an important message for you. It's a matter of life or death! No, not Wife Orbeth! Life! Death! Why is it so hard to send a simple message...

TELEGRAPH

Until the twentieth century, communication between faraway people was either very slow, very basic, or both. Most messages could only travel as fast as the person carrying it.

This fact was particularly troublesome during war. Troop movements, changes in tactics, important news from the government back home: All these messages took so long to reach military commanders, that they might be useless by the time the information was received.

HIGHLIGHTS   Invented by: William Fothergill Cooke and Charles Wheatston

Where There's Smoke There's— a Message?

People in ancient China, Greece, Egypt, and the Americas all used smoke from signal fires as a way to send messages. Drumbeats, reed pipes, and rams' horns were also popular. All these methods were less than perfect. Messages could be messed up by rotten weather, intercepted by enemies, and had to be kept very simple. After all, there's only so much you can say with smoke!

The Arms of the Army

A better communication system, called a semaphore telegraph, was first devised in 1791. A French engineer named Claude Chappe built towers on hilltops between several cities. Each tower had two "arms," like the vanes of a windmill. Each arm could be positioned in seven different ways so that together they made up all the letters of the alphabet. By moving the arms, a messenger at one station could easily send a message to a receiver at the next, and so on. In 1794, the first major line of fifteen stations between Paris and Lille was completed—a message could now travel 200 km (120 mi.) in mere minutes!

Tap Into It

The invention of the battery in 1800 pointed the way to a better communication system. After Hans Christian Oersted proved that an electric current could move a magnetic needle, scientists realized that the needle could be used to tap out a message. Combine this with the idea of sending messages along electrical wires, and you have a much faster delivery method. This is just what William Fothergill Cooke and Charles Wheatstone did in 1837, when they developed an electric telegraph system.

By the end of the nineteenth century, several cables criss-crossed the Atlantic Ocean, which allowed for transatlantic telegraph messages to be sent quickly for the first time.

SPINOFFS

Telegraphs work by sending out codes. The most popular code was developed by American artist Samuel Morse around 1835. Morse learned about electromagnetism, electrical circuits, and batteries and, with his assistant Alfred Vail, came up with a system that used an electromagnet to move a piece of paper under a pen. The pen made a series of dots and dashes on paper—a system that was both fast and easy to use. It became the basis for Morse's great advance, Morse code. By 1837, the Morse and Vail telegraph was ready to launch. It was an instant success and soon replaced the Cooke and Wheatstone system.

It's the Original Instant Message!

Communication was faster and easier thanks to the telegraph. From businesses to the military to newspapers, instant messages were possible for the first time. The telegraph also laid the groundwork for another kind of important invention—the telephone. Hello!

57

No matter how many crops I grow, people seem to need more and more food! To make my harvest even better, I'll need a better...

FERTILIZER

From the earliest days of agriculture, people realized that spreading poop on their fields helped crops grow. Farmers also used burnt weeds, crushed seashells, dead fish, clay, seaweed, even slag left over from making iron to add nutrients to the soil. Although these methods worked, no one knew how to make fertilizers even better.

HIGHLIGHTS Invented by: James Murray and Sir John Lawes When: 184

Plant Learning

The first breakthrough came during the seventeenth century, when German scientist Johann Glauber developed the first artificial mineral fertilizer based on solid scientific research. Scientists were beginning to learn about the nutrients plants needed to grow.

Thanks, Tummyache!

The next breakthrough was caused by, urp, indigestion. In 1817, Irish doctor James Murray set up a factory for his invention, milk of magnesia (used to cure stomach aches). Waste from the factory contained large amounts of phosphorous, an essential plant nutrient. Murray spent years experimenting to find the right formula to turn the waste into something that plants could use so he could sell it as a chemical fertilizer. In 1842 he succeeded, and sold the formula to Sir John Lawes, a wealthy Englishman who had invented a similar fertilizer.

SPINOFFS

The early search for chemical fertilizers led to many chemical compounds that improved our quality of life. One was a painkiller called **aspirin**. Another, **sulfa**, was an antibiotic.

The **ammonia** used to make fertilizers is also a major ingredient for something a little more explosive—**bombs**.

Revolutionizing Agriculture

Lawes's "superphosphate" fertilizers allowed more land to be farmed and more people to be fed. This helped the world's population grow from about one billion people in 1810, to over one and a half billion in 1900, and to more than six billion people today.

The next revolution came after Fritz Haber and Carl Bosch figured out how to make ammonia in a lab in Germany in 1909. The ammonia was added to other synthetic fertilizers, and provided the plants with nitrogen, another important nutrient.

It Grew More Than Just Crops!

Chemical fertilizers greatly increased the amount of food that can be produced and led to population growth. It also spurred the development of the modern chemical industry, which gave us everything from medicine (good) to weapons (bad).

The sun has just set. You're not tired. But with no light except for the fireplace and a smoky candle, you can't read or play a game. You need something to brighten your nights...

LIGHT BULB

In prehistoric times, most people went beddy-bye as soon as the sun slipped below the horizon. About seventy thousand years ago, the first oil lamps began to brighten the family cave. Stones, shells, and bones were hollowed out for bases, while olive, whale, or nut oil were used for fuel.

Most oil lamps, unfortunately, were smoky, stinky, and spooky—their flickers cast weird shadows everywhere. Candles, made from animal fats or beeswax, weren't much better.

The Age of En-light-enment?

There weren't any significant improvements to night lights until the eighteenth century. That's when lamps got glass chimneys to protect the flame and control the flow of air. But they were still pretty dim—and dangerous. House fires were alarmingly common.

It's a Gas!

One alternative to lamp oil was gas. In 1792, Scottish engineer William Murdoch found that he could use the gases produced as a by-product from coal to produce a flame. The flame was much brighter than an oil flame and didn't flicker. Murdoch started a business to sell the gas to factories. The first complete gas-lighting system was installed in an iron foundry in 1802. Gas was a great advance over every other form of lighting. By the middle of the nineteenth century, homes, businesses, even city streets were lit by gas lamps.

Speaking about Gas

Gas has some serious drawbacks. First of all, it can explode. Secondly, it can be toxic to breathe. So scientists kept searching for alternatives.

In 1878, Thomas Edison decided to try developing an electric light bulb. Exploring more than three thousand theories with his colleagues, Edison worked on his bulb for more than a year and a half. The light bulb he finally invented was called the incandescent lamp. It worked by making a strand of carbon so hot that it glowed. The glow gave off a light similar to that of gas, but was steadier in brightness and bluer in tone. Best of all, with no flame and no poisonous gas, the electric light bulb was far safer than gaslight.

Edison also pioneered several other devices essential for a practical electric-lighting system. These included the parallel circuit, safety fuses, and light sockets with on and off switches.

Powering Up

Before homes or businesses could use Edison's electric light bulbs, there had to be a way to make electricity available to everyone. To do this, Edison created a complete system for generating electricity and delivering it to consumers.

In 1882, Edison opened the first commercial power stations in New York City and London. They provided electricity to customers within a 2.6 sq. km (1 sq. mi.) area of the station. The Age of Electricity had begun.

The Night Came Alive!

Not only could people now enjoy the evening hours with more forms of entertainment, they could also work longer. Okay, that's not as exciting, but by adding night shifts, factories could put out goods around the clock.

IN THE DOCTOR'S OFFICE

Pull on your surgical gloves and lab coat—it's time to explore the inside story behind life-saving inventions you'll find in your doctor's examination room.

About a thousand years ago, **hypodermic needles** were invented by Egyptian surgeon Ammar ibn Ali al-Mawsili. He used them to suck a cloudiness called cataracts out of people's eyes! Disposable plastic **syringes** were invented in 1974.

By 200 BCE, people in China had figured out how to prevent people from catching a deadly disease called smallpox. They rubbed powdered scabs from infected people into a small cut on the skin. Without understanding the process, they had invented **vaccination**. In 1796, English scientist Edward Jenner began trying to make a reliable vaccine against smallpox.

Italian scientist Galileo Galilei invented a basic thermometer in 1593. The first medical **thermometer** was invented in 1867 by an English physician, Sir Thomas Allbutt.

Stephen Hales was the first person to measure blood pressure—on a horse! Italian doctor Scipione Riva-Rocci invented the modern **blood pressure gauge** in 1896.

The **Intravenous Drip system**, or **IV**, was invented by Justine Wanger and her colleagues in 1931. An IV allowed vital fluids to be steadily injected into a patient's veins. Before becoming a scientist, Wanger was an actress.

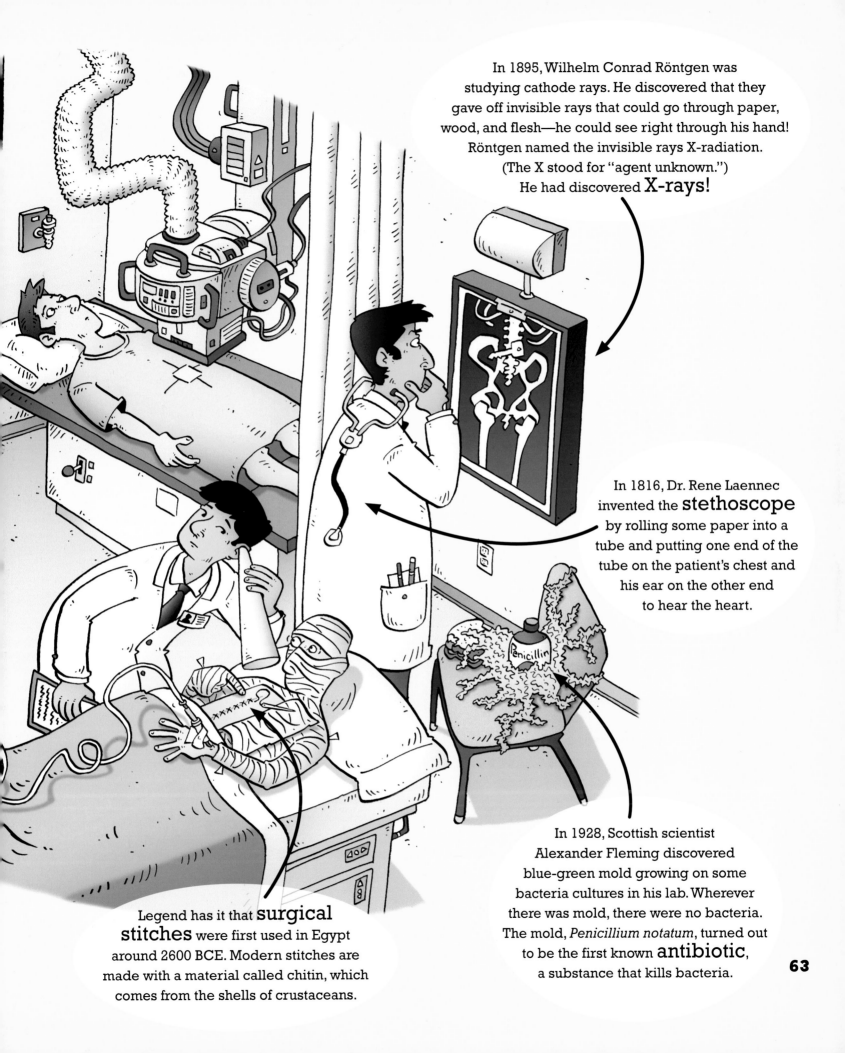

In 1895, Wilhelm Conrad Röntgen was studying cathode rays. He discovered that they gave off invisible rays that could go through paper, wood, and flesh—he could see right through his hand! Röntgen named the invisible rays X-radiation. (The X stood for "agent unknown.") He had discovered **X-rays**!

In 1816, Dr. Rene Laennec invented the **stethoscope** by rolling some paper into a tube and putting one end of the tube on the patient's chest and his ear on the other end to hear the heart.

In 1928, Scottish scientist Alexander Fleming discovered blue-green mold growing on some bacteria cultures in his lab. Wherever there was mold, there were no bacteria. The mold, *Penicillium notatum*, turned out to be the first known **antibiotic**, a substance that kills bacteria.

Legend has it that **surgical stitches** were first used in Egypt around 2600 BCE. Modern stitches are made with a material called chitin, which comes from the shells of crustaceans.

Not so Long Ago...

From Paper to Screen

During the twentieth century, new inventions continued to bring change to the world. Television gave people a new way to obtain information and entertainment. Automobiles let people live farther away from where they worked, in new housing areas called suburbs. Telephones allowed people to communicate easily from anywhere in the world.

Meanwhile, just out of sight of ordinary people, another revolution was getting started. It involved how information was collected and stored. Since the invention of paper in the second century CE, the way people recorded things had not changed much. Anything of importance was written on paper that was then assembled into books.

But by the start of the twentieth century, people had found a new way to record information. Instead of printed words, this method used punched holes to create a numerical, or digital, code that was read by a computer. Computers could do calculations faster and share data more easily than ever. The Digital Revolution had begun.

This massive revolution is still going on today—you are smack in the middle of it! What will the next wave of inventions be? No one knows for sure, but you can count on life being radically different twenty years from now!

Sure, steam engines are totally hot with **big** businesses, but you still need your cranky old horse to pull your wagon. When will someone invent an engine for the little guy?

ENGINE

Even way back in the eighteenth century, scientists reasoned an internal combustion engine—one in which fuel could be burned right inside the engine—would waste less energy than a steam engine. Steam engines are great for providing power on a large scale but, because their fuel (usually coal) is located outside the engine in a separate compartment, a lot of energy gets wasted.

HIGHLIGHTS Invented by: Eugenio Barsanti   When: 1856   Where: Ita

The Car(riage) Race Is On!

In 1854, an Italian priest named Eugenio Barsanti was the first to invent a working internal combustion engine. It used coal gas for fuel. Unfortunately, Barsanti caught typhoid fever and died without ever learning everything that his engine could—and would—do.

Engine Driver

In 1860, Belgian engineer Jean Joseph Étienne Lenoir invented his own version of the internal combustion engine. The real advance came when he attached his engine to a carriage frame. With a single stroke, Lenoir had invented the car!

Otto's Auto Engine

In 1868, two Germans named Nikolaus Otto and Eugen Langen started a business making engines similar to Lenoir's. But Otto was not satisfied with how the engines worked. They were noisy and wasted a lot of energy. So he came up with a better design of his own in 1876. The engine, called the Otto-cycle engine, is still the basic design for most car and truck engines today.

The First Gasoline Engines

Gottlieb Daimler was a scientist who worked for Nikolaus Otto. The two men had a falling out and Daimler was fired. Daimler decided to start his own business.

Up until then, the fuel for internal combustion engines came from various sources—hydrogen, coal gas, or kerosene. Daimler decided to try a different fuel: gasoline. With his partner Wilhem Maybach, they came up with an internal combustion engine that was seven times faster than previous models.

Daimler and Maybach's gasoline engine, when placed in a stagecoach, allowed it to travel at the hair-raising speed of 18 km (11 mi.) per hour. It was now only a matter of time before cars, powered by internal combustion engines, would completely replace the horse-drawn carriage.

How Internal Combustion Engines Work

1. A mixture of fuel and air is sprayed into a cylinder.
2. A second cylinder, called a piston, slides into the first cylinder. It pushes down on the air and fuel, compressing it.
3. An electrical pulse travels through a device called a spark plug. When an electric circuit closes, the spark plug releases a spark. The spark ignites the fuel inside the cylinder.
4. The explosion forces the piston out of the cylinder. As the piston moves, it turns a crank that can perform work, such as turning the wheels of a car.

Steps 1 to 4 repeat over and over again!

They Really Took Us For a Ride!

Simply put, without the internal combustion engine, there would be no cars, trucks, or airplanes to move people and goods around the world. Man, would that ever change a lot of things!

Wow! Look at all these orders. It seems like everyone wants a car. Too bad none of these cars is, you know, built yet...

CAR

In the early days, every car was custom made. This was an expensive and slow process. In 1894, carmaker Karl Benz decided to offer only a single standard car model. It was called the Velocipede, or Velo. The Velo could be built much faster, and at a cheaper price, than custom-made cars. They became so popular that twelve hundred were sold from 1894 to 1901, a huge number for the time.

HIGHLIGHTS   Invented by: Jean Joseph Étienne Lenoir   When: 1860

A Mass-ive Idea

By the turn of the twentieth century, gasoline-powered cars were outselling all other types of vehicles. The market was growing, and there was money to be made by anyone able to meet the demand for cheap, reliable cars.

Back in 1798, American inventor Eli Whitney pioneered a manufacturing technique called mass production. Goods were made in large numbers using identical machine-made parts. His speedy method was first used to make muskets, but was also adopted by bicycle makers.

Ford-ging Ahead

That's how an American bicycle mechanic named Henry Ford became familiar with the idea of mass production. *Why not use that same technique to build cars?* he thought. Ford set up a factory in Highland Park, Michigan. His workers were arranged in an assembly line, where each was responsible for performing a single task. In 1913, he put the cars on a conveyor belt. The belt automatically moved cars from worker to worker, saving time and labor.

Using the new method, Ford's car, called the Model T, could be assembled in an incredible ninety-three minutes. By 1927, Ford had built fifteen million Model T's, making the Ford Company the world's leading carmaker.

SPINOFFS

In 1903, Mary Anderson noticed that streetcar drivers couldn't see when it rained. They would have to open the windows. So she invented the **windshield wiper.** (Early models were hand-powered.) By 1916, the wipers were standard features on every American car!

The first **crash test dummy**, named Sierra Sam, was invented in 1949. Human drivers around the world say, "Thank you!"

They got us around!

Cars gave people more freedom than they could have ever imagined. Cars also meant building modern paved roadways, the creation of suburban communities around large cities, and more frequent visits to your aunt's house.

Where: France

A telegraph is handy and all, but wouldn't it be better if people could actually hear each other talking, instead of dashing to the telegraph office to send dotty messages?

TELEPHONE

Mr. Watson, come here, I want you!

As soon as the telegraph was invented in 1837, people began to imagine a version of the device that would transmit human voices instead of coded messages. In 1860, German scientist Johann Philipp Reis came up with a working voice transmitter made from a sausage skin, a barrel bung, and a violin case! Not surprisingly, Reis's transmitter was unreliable and did not produce good quality sound. He never tried to patent it and considered it a toy, not a useful communication device.

Ringing My Bell

In 1874, inventor Alexander Graham Bell decided to work on voice transmission. He knew that humans heard when vibrations made by sound waves reached the eardrum. His challenge was to make sound into pulses of electricity, then create an artificial eardrum to catch the sounds. Afterward, he would need to convert the pulses back into sound waves.

Whoops! A Happy Accident

Bell hired an electrician, Thomas Watson, as his assistant. They set up a test of their invention, with the "transmitter" (to send sound) in Bell's room and the "receiver" (to catch sound) in Watson's room. Bell pressed a key attached to a reed. When the reed was touched, it was supposed to vibrate at a particular pitch. That note was then to travel via electrical wires to the receiver. There, a reed in the receiver would begin vibrating at the same speed, making an identical sound.

Except, it didn't.

Bell thought the reed might have gotten stuck, so Watson touched it with his finger to set it free. At that moment, the reed in Bell's transmitter began to vibrate! The receiver had become the transmitter! Bell was able to figure it out. Later that night he wrote in a letter, "I have accidentally made a discovery of the very greatest importance."

Spills and Thrills

While the two men were getting closer to their goal of being able to transmit human voices, the results were not clear enough to be practical. Then one day, Bell spilled acid on himself during an experiment. He spoke into his invention, "Mr. Watson, come here. I want you!" Watson heard Bell clearly through the receiver and came running.

Thanks to Bell's lucky accident, they had just had the first phone conversation! Funnily enough, after Bell became famous for inventing the telephone, he refused to have a telephone in his study. He said its ringing interrupted his work!

SPINOFFS

In 1973, American inventor Martin Cooper freed phones from landlines when he invented the first practical **cellular telephone**. According to Cooper, the inspiration for his mobile phone was the hand-held communicators used by characters in the TV series *Star Trek*!

Canadian inventor Mike Lazaridis, owner of the company Research in Motion (RIM), invented the **BlackBerry** in 1999. The palm-sized portable device was not only a phone, it could also send and receive email and surf the net. At the time, there was nothing else like it.

Answering the Call

Eventually, the telephone would offer real-time voice communication between people around the world. It was also the foundation for technology that helped develop the computer and the Internet.

BIGTHINKERS

Inventions: Telephone, metal detector, hydrofoils, many more

Alexander Graham Bell

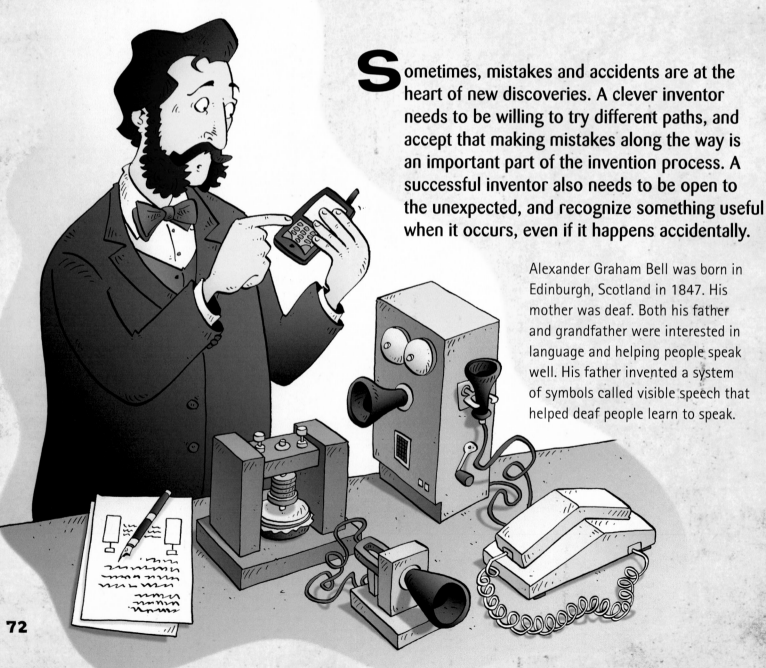

Sometimes, mistakes and accidents are at the heart of new discoveries. A clever inventor needs to be willing to try different paths, and accept that making mistakes along the way is an important part of the invention process. A successful inventor also needs to be open to the unexpected, and recognize something useful when it occurs, even if it happens accidentally.

Alexander Graham Bell was born in Edinburgh, Scotland in 1847. His mother was deaf. Both his father and grandfather were interested in language and helping people speak well. His father invented a system of symbols called visible speech that helped deaf people learn to speak.

The young Bell gets to work.

Twenty years later...

Look What's Talking

As a child, Bell learned about how people produce the sounds of speech. When he was just fourteen, he and his brother made an artificial talking head using a tin tube, rubber, and the larynx (voice box) of a dead lamb. By blowing into the tube, they could make the head "speak."

Sit, Fido! Speak, Fido!

Bell also liked to goof around with his family's terrier. Using what he knew about vocal cords, he figured out how to press on the dog's throat and make it "speak" the words, "How are you, grandmamma?" There's no record of how the dog felt about this experiment.

I Just Don't Get It

When Bell was sixteen, an expert on language suggested that he read a book about the experiments of a German scientist named Hermann von Helmholtz. The book described how Helmholtz had used electric wires connected to tuning forks to make sounds.

Bell didn't understand German or know anything about electricity, so when he read the book, he misunderstood it. Bell thought that Helmholtz had sent the sounds through the wires as a telegraph sent Morse code signals through wires. That boo-boo got Bell's brain buzzing. What if he could send the sound of a person's voice across long distances using electricity?

Bell in Boston

While working as a teacher of the deaf in Boston, Massachusetts, Bell met some rich backers who agreed to support him in a venture to design an improved telegraph.

While doing research, Bell had an idea that took him in a new direction. He called his invention a "phonautograph." This machine picked up sounds and turned them into written symbols. The part that picked up the sound was a dead man's ear!

Bell asked himself: Could he create an artificial vibrating "eardrum" that would use an electric current to make the pulses? This was the idea that led directly to his major success—the telephone.

Up, Up and Away

Thanks to the telephone, Bell achieved great wealth and fame, but that did not stop him from exploring new ideas. In 1907, he formed a firm with four engineers called the Aerial Experiment Association. They designed and built an airplane called the *Silver Dart*, which made the first powered flight in Canada in 1909.

Alexander continued inventing until he died in 1922. His inventions include, among many others, the hydrofoil boat, a metal detector, and the fiber optics that are used in telecommunications devices such as the Internet and cell phones.

Using the phone, you can only send your message to one person at a time. Wouldn't it be nice if you could talk to many listeners at once?

RADIO

In 1864, Scottish scientist James Clerk Maxwell made a prediction: One day, high frequency waves (radio waves) will be used to transmit messages. Soon a fierce competition began between scientists such as Nikola Tesla and Heinrich Hertz as they rushed to make the prediction come true.

HIGHLIGHTS   Invented by: Guglielmo Marconi   When: 1901   Where

The Mark of Marconi

A young Italian named Guglielmo Marconi was captivated by news of these experiments. He began to conduct experiments of his own. In 1895, when he was just twenty-one, Marconi succeeded in sending his first wireless messages from his house to a receiver on the other side of a hill.

Marconi had an obsessive streak. He worked non-stop on his invention. He soon put together an entire system that was able to send simple messages using Morse code. He couldn't find anyone to support his work in Italy, so he moved to Great Britain. There, he was given a helping hand by the Chief Electrical Engineer of the British Post Office, William Preece. Preece introduced Marconi and his wireless telegraph at a lecture at the Royal Institution of Great Britain in 1897. Marconi became an overnight celebrity.

Making All Kinds of Waves

In one exciting demonstration, Marconi sent signals across the English Channel. He made history in 1901 when he sent the first wireless message across the Atlantic Ocean. These events made Marconi's wireless telegraph extremely popular, especially at sea. It was also used instead of a telegraph as a communication device between individuals.

One problem with radio waves is that they were tricky to detect. In 1906, Lee de Forest, an American physicist, invented a device that solved this problem. He created an amplifier that made it easier to generate and hear radio signals. With de Forest's amplitude modulating (AM, for short) transmitter, radio signals could now be broadcast to many people at once—to anyone, in fact, who had a radio receiver. De Forest was also the first person to use the word "radio."

Casting a Net into the Radio Waves

In 1900, Reginald Fessenden sent the first radio transmission of the human voice. On Christmas Eve 1906, he broadcast the first radio show. Sailors at sea off the Massachusetts coast were flabbergasted to hear Fessenden playing the violin and reading from the Bible. The modern era of radio was born.

SPIN OFFS

When Thomas Edison designed his electric light, he created a vacuum inside a glass bulb by sucking all the air out of it. This helped the light shine brighter. At the same time, he discovered that the vacuum let him detect electrons that flowed through it. This finding came to be known as the Edison effect. De Forest's amplifiers took advantage of the Edison effect. They were called vacuum tubes and were also used in early radios, televisions, and amplifiers for musical instruments.

The Whole World Was Listening

Radio allowed for long distance communication without using wires or cables. Families could huddle around their radio to hear news from around the world. It also let captains on boats and planes stay in touch in case of emergencies.

Telephones are grand. Radio is divine. But a picture's worth a thousand words...

TELEVISION

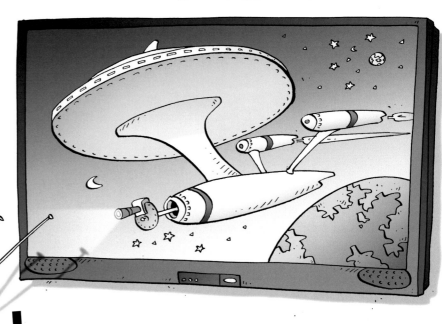

In 1873, a telegraph operator named Joseph May was experimenting with metals to find a semi-conductor—a substance that conducted electricity, but not very well.

May noticed that selenium conducted electricity far better in sunlight than in the dark. That got him thinking. What if you shone light in a pattern onto selenium? Could that pattern—e.g., a picture—then be sent along a wire by electrical impulses, much as a telegraph message was sent?

In 1884, researcher Paul Nipkow built on May's idea. He projected an image onto a disk that had holes punched into it in a regular pattern. On the other side of the disk was a selenium-coated sensor. When the disk spun, light passed through the holes and onto the sensor in ring-shaped patterns of light and dark. The sensor converted the patterns into electrical impulses. The "Nipkow disk" worked, but its impulses were very weak. They needed to be amplified to be useful.

76

Fax it to My TV

In 1881, Shelford Bidwell used the Nipkow disk to send photographs—sort of like a fax machine. It was 1923, however, before anyone could send moving pictures. Those images were simple black silhouettes on a white background.

In 1926, a British inventor named John Logie Baird unveiled the first functional television system. It used a Nipkow disk and worked well enough to produce a recognizable human face on the other end. But his television needed a lot of light to work and could only produce very small, fuzzy pictures.

They Needed a Ray Gun

At around the same time that May and Nipkow were experimenting with selenium and spinning disks, other scientists were fiddling with vacuums. One of these vacuum-crazy scientists was William Crookes. Around 1875, he designed a vacuum tube called the Crookes tube. With it, he produced a mysterious stream of energy he called cathode rays. Crookes didn't know what the rays were, but he showed that they traveled in straight lines and caused the objects they hit to glow.

Electronic Television

In 1897, J.J. Thomson discovered that cathode rays were actually fast-moving streams of atomic particles called electrons.

Karl Ferdinand Braun, a German physicist, used an alternating current—electricity that flowed first one way and then the other—to shoot a narrow beam of electrons from one end of the tube. The beam traced a pattern on a fluorescent screen that had been painted at the other end. He called his invention a cathode ray tube (CRT).

Fourteen-year-old American teenager Philo Farnsworth realized that electron beams—if they traveled back and forth across an image—could instantly draw a picture of what they scanned. Six years later, Farnsworth invented a system that used only electronic components, like a CRT, to convert electrical impulses into light. He had invented the TV.

By the end of the 1930s, electronic TV had taken over as the most popular form of television. But TVs were very expensive. It wasn't until the 1950s that they became affordable to most people.

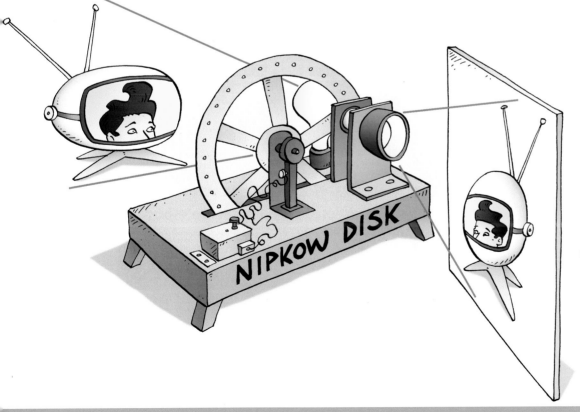

NIPKOW DISK

One in Every Home...or Two or Three?

TV has had a massive influence on, well, everything! The way people understand the world, entertain themselves, and even how they dress, speak, and behave is related to TV.

77

You've got to get from town X to town Z. Unfortunately, mountain Y lies in-between. Going around it will take forever. If only you could fly over it like a bird!

AIRPLANE

Wright Flyer

Most early attempts to fly tried to copy the flapping of a bird's wings. None got off the ground. That's because human arms are simply not strong enough to power an artificial wing, no matter how light.

In the nineteenth century, scientists and inventors branched out in new directions. Some of their ideas were plain crazy. One plane was launched with a giant spring! Others were deadly. Many early aviators died in crashes and falls. Nevertheless, by 1900, several inventors were close to success.

HIGHLIGHTS   Invented by: Orville and Wilbur Wright   When: 1903

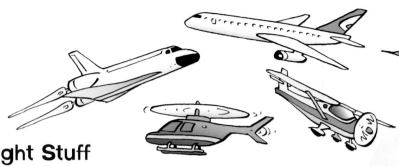

The Wright Stuff

In 1896, brothers Wilbur and Orville Wright read how German inventor Otto Lilienthal had died in a glider crash. Wilbur suspected that the reason behind Lilienthal's accident was that he'd had no controls in his glider. That made Wilbur decide that figuring out how to control his own flyer would be his top priority.

For the Birds

As he studied the problem, Wilbur watched birds. Finally, he concluded that birds controlled their flight with twists of their wings that changed their shape and position. But how could Wilbur twist the stiff wings of an aircraft? He puzzled over the problem for years without any clue of how to solve it.

Twist and Shout Hurray!

One day, Wilbur came across a long, narrow box that had held a bicycle tire's inner tube from his bicycle shop. He twisted the box. One end turned up, and the other turned down. This was the trick Wilbur needed for his glider wings!

Up, Up and Away

The Wrights knew that to achieve liftoff, they would need a steadier wind than was common around their hometown of Dayton, Ohio. So they headed to a long strip of windy beach at Kitty Hawk, North Carolina to test their latest glider designs. In 1902, they finished building the engine and added it to the *Flyer*, the largest airplane they had ever built. It measured 9.8 m (32 ft.) from wing tip to wing tip.

On December 17, 1903, Orville climbed into the cockpit. Twelve seconds later, the impossible dream had come true. The Wrights had achieved flight!

The Skies Became a Lot Friendlier

The airplane made travel faster than ever before and broke down barriers—oceans, mountains, and long distances were soon no match for it! Plus, from the development of the airplane came big innovations like space travel and communications satellites.

Where: United States

Wouldn't it be great if you could just mix a few ingredients together and—POOF!—you could make whatever you wanted, whenever you wanted it? It's not magic, it's...

PLASTIC

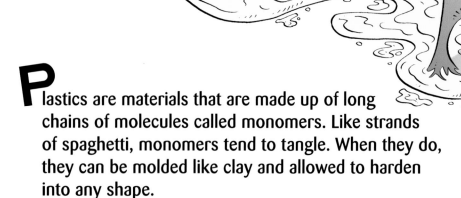

Plastics are materials that are made up of long chains of molecules called monomers. Like strands of spaghetti, monomers tend to tangle. When they do, they can be molded like clay and allowed to harden into any shape.

Believe it or not, there are a few natural plastics in the world. Shellac is a shiny, hard coating made from scale insects (used to make buttons and the first phonograph records); ebonite, a hard form of rubber (used to make bowling balls); and gutta-percha, the sap from a tropical tree (used for furniture and to insulate telegraph cables).

HIGHLIGHTS Invented by: Alexander Parkes   When: 1855   Where: Gre

Plastic Tusks?

During the Industrial Revolution, scientists and inventors the world over were experimenting with new ways to make familiar objects. British chemist Alexander Parkes decided to try and create a replacement for ivory. At the time, ivory was popular, but it was also expensive. Parkes believed he could make a lot of money with an artificial replacement for elephant tusks.

Leftover Gunk

One day, Parkes noticed an old jar of collodion at the back of his medicine chest. Collodion was a mixture of cotton and chemicals that was used to cover wounds. Parkes's jar had dried up, leaving a moldable gunk at the bottom. Parkes mixed the collodion with acids and oils. It made a dough that could be molded, textured, carved, and painted to look just like ivory, and many other materials as well. He called it Parkesine. Sadly, nobody thought that Parkesine was as cool and useful as Parkes did. It was too hard and prone to cracking. His company went bust.

The Exploding Billiard Ball

An American named John Wesley Hyatt also wanted to invent a substitute for ivory. His invention, called celluloid, was similar to Parkesine, but not as hard. He used it to make billiard balls. Unfortunately, celluloid had a bad habit of catching fire under impact. When the balls smashed into each other, they exploded!

But when handled properly, celluloid worked well. It was an excellent substitute for amber or tortoiseshell, which was used for making jewelry and combs. Celluloid was also used to make film for photography and motion pictures.

The Material of a Thousand Uses

Synthetic plastics made a big step forward in 1907. A chemist named Leo Baekeland had the goal of developing a replacement for shellac. His creation, Bakelite, was made from a mixture of two chemicals: formaldehyde (embalming fluid) and phenol (made from coal tar).

The resulting goop was resistant to heat. It could be added to other materials, like wood, to make them stronger. It could be molded into any shape, made in any color, and used for dozens of purposes: toilet seats, airplane parts, telephones, insulators, beads, engine valves, and more. Bakelite became known as "the material of a thousand uses."

During the Second World War, demand for Bakelite surged. The U.S. military used it for everything from cutlery for soldiers to parts in the atomic bomb!

Is There Anything Plastic Can't Do? Oh Yeah, Break Down...

Because plastics were both cheap and versatile, they could be used to make previously unimaginable things. By the 1970s, more plastic was being produced per year than iron and steel. Unfortunately, this material cannot break down naturally. This has led to excessive amounts of plastic waste in the world.

IN THE KITCHEN

With much more food now available, it was no surprise that people also looked for ways to improve devices found in the kitchen. Many of these labor-saving devices were dreamed up by women.

The first **dishwasher**, invented in 1850, was a hand-turned wheel that splashed water on dishes. Unfortunately, it did more splashing than washing. In 1886, American socialite Josephine Cochran invented a much better dishwasher.

Invented in 1679 by French physicist Denis Papin, "Papin's Digester" was a **pressure cooker** that produced hot food more quickly than conventional cooking methods. The device inspired the invention of the steam engine.

American factory worker Charles Strite was sick of eating burnt toast in his company's cafeteria. So in 1919, he invented a machine to do the job right. The **pop-up toaster** used both a timer and springs to make the toast pop into the air when it was perfectly cooked.

British scientist Harry Brearley invented **stainless steel knives** and **forks** by accident when he was trying to invent a new material for making rifles!

American engineer Lillian Gilbreth invented the **step-on lever trash can** in the 1940s. She also designed a model kitchen for use by the disabled, as well as the **electric mixer**.

In 1913, an engineer named Jesse Littleton brought home a heat-resistant glass container he used at work to hold battery acid. His wife baked a cake in it, inventing a new use for the product. She is known to history as "the **Pyrex** housewife."

The **recloseable cereal box** was invented by Mary Spaeth at the age of eight! When she grew up, she invented the **barcode scanner** for the U.S. military.

During World War II, the British were experimenting with devices that gave off radiation. A technician named Dr. Percy Spencer accidentally discovered that the radiation could heat foods when a bar of chocolate that had been in his pocket melted. From this bittersweet boo-boo, the **microwave** oven was born.

Arthur Scott was the head of a large paper company. One day in 1907, he received a shipment of paper that was too thick to be used as toilet paper as intended. The paper roll was perforated into towel-sized sheets and used in public washrooms. In 1931, Scott began selling rolls of **paper towels** for use in homes.

American chemist Mary Engle Pennington invented several processes for freezing fruits, vegetables, and fish during the early 1900s. American inventor Clarence Birdseye, another **frozen food** innovator, got his ideas for quick-freezing food from Inuit people while living in Labrador, Canada.

Counting olives is no fun when you've got gazillions of them. If only there were a tool that made these large computations quickly! I think I'd call it a...

COMPUTER

In the 1800s, the word computer meant a person who computes, or does calculations. (They were mostly women.) It really bugged a mathematician named Charles Babbage that the computers made mistakes, so he worked with a woman named Ada Lovelace to develop a machine called the analytical engine. Powered by a steam engine, it both calculated numbers and stored the results using punch cards. Although it was never finished, Babbage's creation is recognized as the first true digital computer.

Cool, Calculating Warriors

The next advance in the calculating machine was the Hollerith desk, which could read the holes punched in cards. It was invented by Herman Hollerith to help tabulate the results of the 1890 census. He later founded the IBM computer company.

Pest Control

During World War II, the U.S. military constructed Mark I, a massive computer that could do complex calculations. One of the main programmers of Mark I was Grace Hopper. She also wrote the first high-level computer language (one that made sense to people) and invented the compiler, a computer program that turns commands into a language the computer can understand. One day the Mark I stopped working properly. Hopper found a dead moth in the machine that was blocking the holes in the paper read-out. She pulled the bug out to repair the machine, becoming the first person to debug a computer!

Going Digital

Much like early TVs, the computer's mechanical parts didn't work as well as its electronic ones. In 1945, Americans John Mauchly, a scientist, and J. Presper Eckert, an engineer, built the first completely electronic digital computer. It used eighteen thousand vacuum tubes and weighed 27,000 kg (60,000 lbs.)!

Burn Outs

By the 1960s, number-crunching computers were being used all over the world. But they were huge, hot, and costly to operate. The problem lay in the vacuum tubes. They were unreliable and, like light bulbs, they burned out. A single burnt-out tube would shut the whole computer down.

It's Wafer Thin!

Transistors began replacing vacuum tubes in the late 1950s. They were much smaller, more reliable, and did not give off heat. In 1959, Robert Noyce and Jack Kilby each independently invented devices called integrated circuits, that allowed hundreds of transistors to be placed on a tiny wafer of silicon. With the ability to store information in such petite packages, the computer got smaller and more powerful every year.

FIRST TRYS

The **abacus** was invented thousands of years ago. It used beads to help people add and subtract quickly.

In the 1600s, the **slide rule** was devised. This ruler had movable parts that let the user multiply and divide like lightning! It didn't give precise answers or record information, but it was the main tool of engineers until calculators were invented.

The punch cards used by early computers were an improvement on a weaver's invention. In 1801, Joseph-Marie Jacquard invented the **Jacquard loom**, which was fitted with a roll of cards punched with holes. When connected together, the cards acted as a set of instructions for the pattern on the cloth.

According to my Calculations

Computers made complicated calculations a snap, and that led to huge leaps in problem-solving for the world's thinkers. Plus, vital information could now be stored in new versatile ways.

By 1970, large computers were found in corporations and governments around the world—awesome!—but they were the size of a small room—bummer! People, can we work on this size thing?

PERSONAL COMPUTER

By 1971, the integrated circuit was taken one giant step further to become the microprocessor. A microprocessor is a tiny chip of silicon that acts as thousands of integrated circuits rolled into one. Thanks to this invention, one teensy chip could hold more information and process data faster than any previous computer component.

HIGHLIGHTS   Invented by: Many, many people   When: Mid-1970s

Opening the Flood Gates

In 1975, Harvard University student Bill Gates and a friend started a company called Microsoft to write software for a kind of computer that didn't even exist yet—the personal computer, or PC. In 1980, they were approached by computer giant IBM to write software for a new line of PCs that IBM was developing. Gates wrote a text-only operating system called MS-DOS, short for "Microsoft Disk Operating System." Thanks to MS-DOS, IBM's PC became a smash hit. Suddenly, everyone wanted one.

Taking a Bite out of IBM?

In 1976, Steve Jobs started a company with his friend Steve Wozniak and investor Mike Markkula to make and sell their own computers. They named the company Apple. One of the original features of the first Apple computer was that it had a TV for display—most other computers had no display at all! The TV only displayed text, though, and it was really slow.

A Very Gooey Problem

One day, an electrical engineer named Douglas Engelbart had a flash of insight while driving to work. Engelbart envisioned a way that cathode ray tubes (CRTs) could be used by a computer to display information as easy-to-understand pictures.

In 1968, twenty years after he first had the idea, Engelbart unveiled his concept. It included the first mouse and a GUI—an acronym for graphical user interface. The GUI allowed users to view pictures on the screen.

Jobs hired some engineers who had worked on the GUI to team up with Apple's programmers. Thanks to the GUI, Apple's Macintosh computers included the first easy-to-manipulate icons, such as files you could drag and drop into trash cans.

Opening the Window(s)

Apple computers were a huge success. Compared to MS-DOS, the Mac operating system was easy to use. Microsoft launched its own GUI operating system, Windows, in 1985. Whether users preferred Macs or PCs, one thing was certain: Personal computers were here to stay.

It's the Little Chip That Did!

The PC—and its microprocessors—brought incredible computing power to how we work, play, and communicate. What's more, everything from cars to toasters now uses microchip technology.

Where: United States

BIGTHINKERS

Inventions: Personal computers and software programs

Steve Jobs & Bill Gates

Sometimes, becoming a trailblazer rests on having fabulous timing. Bill Gates and Steve Jobs were not only blessed with brains, talent, and ambition, but were interested in the right technology at the right time. Using the talents of people around them with similar interests in computers, both men became billionaires.

Birth of the Computer Age

Buying Computer Time

Bill Gates was born in Seattle, Washington in 1955. When he was thirteen years old, his school obtained access to computers for the students. Gates and his friend Paul Allen fell in love with computers. They began spending all their free time writing programs for them. By the following autumn, Gates and his pals were spending so much time on the computers at the lab that they caused the expensive equipment to crash!

By the age of fifteen, Gates was both earning money from his programming skills and becoming one of the most experienced computer programmers in the country. Two years after starting a company called Microsoft in 1975, Gates dropped out of college.

Time for Success

Gates was a whiz at programming, but he was also a crack businessman. In his deal with IBM (see page 87), he made sure he kept the rights to MS-DOS. When MS-DOS became the most popular operating system in the world, Gates became the richest man in the world.

Steve Jobs

Steve Jobs was born in San Francisco, California in 1955. While still in junior high school in nearby Cupertino, he grew interested in the brand-new field of computer science. Jobs began going to lectures after school that were given by the computer firm Hewlett Packard. He and another student named Steve Wozniak were hired as summer employees.

Time to Explore

Jobs was not much of a student. He left college after only one term and began working at Atari, a video game pioneer. Later, he started Apple with Wozniak and Mike Markkula. They not only made and sold computers, they created the software that allowed the computer to perform various tasks, too. Early computers were difficult for most people to operate. Jobs understood that a more attractive, easier-to-use computer would appeal to the average person. Apple soon became Microsoft's biggest competitor, a rivalry that continues today.

You've got lots of computers chock full of data. But what if you're attacked by an enemy? You need a way to move that precious data safely before a bomb drops on it!

INTERNET

In 1962, a professor at the Massachusetts Institute of Technology (MIT) named J.C.R. Licklider, came up with the concept of a "Galactic Network." He imagined a network of computers around the world that were connected so that everyone could share information. Two years later, the American military embarked on a plan to store important data in different locations. The project was called the Advanced Research Projects Agency Network—ARPAnet for short. It built on Licklider's ideas.

HIGHLIGHTS Invented by: Vinton Cerf When: 1973 Where: United State

The Old Switcheroo

For ARPAnet to work, an effective way for computers to communicate with one another was needed. ARPAnet's Chief Scientist, Lawrence Roberts, came up with packet switching, which split up large data into smaller units. This allowed many users to send messages via the same wires at the same time, greatly increasing the speed of communication. Using packet switching, the first four ARPAnet computers were connected to each other in 1969.

Cerf's Up!

Vinton Cerf was one of the team of computer scientists who figured out how to get ARPAnet computers to talk to each other. By 1973, Cerf had already begun designing a better method. With an electrical engineer named Robert Kahn, Cerf came up with an innovative system called Transmission Control Protocol/Internet Protocol (TCP/IP). It worked far better than the original system and allowed any computer to share data with any other computer over an ordinary telephone line. From this, the Internet was born.

The World Wide Wow!

In 1991, British computer scientist Timothy Berners-Lee posted the software he developed for the World Wide Web on the Internet. Computer enthusiasts around the world used the free software and began setting up their own servers. Here are the steps Berners-Lee took to create the Web:

1. Create software with a key feature called hypertext. Hypertext allowed users to jump from one entry or document to another by way of links.
2. Come up with a way to identify and locate different Internet documents using an address, or URL. (e.g., http://www.helainebecker.com).
3. Develop software that allows a computer to store information for an Internet page or site—server software.
4. Write a program for a browser—software that would allow you to search and use documents prepared with hypertext.

Whoa! Is It Me, or Did the World Get a Lot Smaller?

Whether it was for a big business meeting or a little conversation with a friend in Brazil, the Internet was a huge invention. Text, music, videos, and pictures could be shared with people around the world as though they sat right beside you!

Records, cassette tapes, CDs—all clunky forms of audio storage to lug around. If only you could carry around tons of your fave tunes anywhere you liked!

MP3

HIGHLIGHTS Invented by: Several people, most notably Karlheinz Brandenbu

B ack in 1877, Thomas Edison invented the phonograph, which could record and play back sounds. It had a rotating cylinder wrapped in tin foil. Sound vibrations caused a needle, or stylus, to etch a wavy line into the foil as the cylinder turned, making a record of the sounds. When you turned the cylinder again, those sounds played back.

Edison's phonograph was improved on by many other inventors. Instead of needing to go to a concert hall to hear music, people could listen in the comfort of their homes. By 1912, most records were no longer made on cylinders, but on flat disks called platters. These disks broke often, so they were replaced by more durable vinyl records. Vinyl was an improvement, but still scratched easily.

CDs Seize the Day

In 1982, Philips Industries introduced the compact disc, or CD. CDs actually recorded sounds in much the same way as Edison's foil cylinders, except that the grooves were etched with, and then read by, a laser. This technique made the CDs' sound much sharper and clearer than the old vinyl records. CDs were also smaller, cheaper, and less likely to scratch or warp than vinyl records.

Computer Revolution

In 1977, German professor Dieter Seitzer began working on a way to send music over phone lines. Mathematics and electronics specialist Karlheinz Brandenburg was part of his research team. Their problem was that sound files are large. If they could be squeezed, or compressed, into smaller files, then music could be manipulated, transferred, and played more easily. The team's biggest challenge was squishing the files without sacrificing sound quality. It took ten long years to achieve their goal! In 1989, Brandenburg revealed their record-smashing invention—the MP3 file. The new software meant audio files, on average, were about one-tenth their original size. Researchers continue to improve the size and quality of music files offered by MP3.

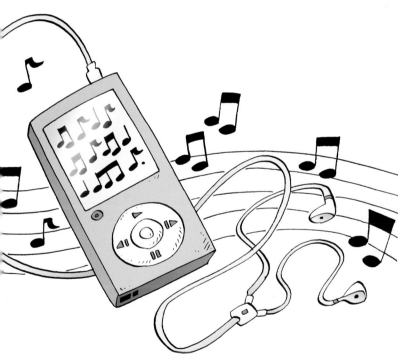

I've Got a DJ on My Hip!

MP3s allowed large audio files to be made into a more manageable size. This is the technology that allows you to carry your entire music collection in your back pocket. That's handy!

WHAT'S NEXT?

We've come a long way, and new inventions are appearing all the time. As we continue to build on inventions of the past, no one can say for sure what the future will bring. It is clear that they will all, in some new way, fill our basic human needs. Each of these fascinating inventions is already on some inventor's drawing board.

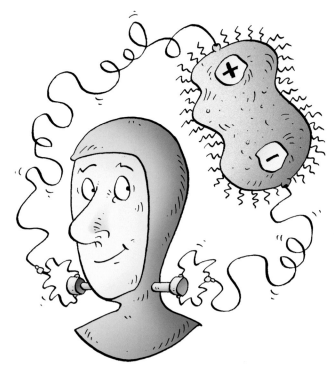

Feeling Low on Energy?

Consider powering up with tiny batteries put together by viruses! These barely-there batteries are about half the size of a human cell. According to researchers, the puny power sources may one day be integrated into living organisms—like us.

Spray-on Sweater

Skin-tight would take on a whole new meaning with a spray-on sweater. This new chemical is designed to turn into a cloud of non-woven cloth when sprayed onto the skin. Once in place, you can style the fabric into any design you like—no sewing needles needed!

Bacto-bananas? Glow-wheat?

Farming and better fertilizers are not enough to feed Earth's growing population. Genetic engineering combines the best qualities of one plant with features of...well...just about anything. Genetically modified corn, tomatoes, and soybeans are already grown in large quantities. Some of the new crops under development will offer more nutrition, better pest control, and larger yields.

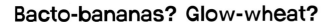

No More Casualties

Someday soon, soldiers on the battlefield may be a thing of the past. In the meantime, however, a device resembling the cuff of a blood pressure gauge is being developed that will fit on the arm or leg of a wounded soldier and give off ultrasound waves to speed healing. This will allow soldiers to recover from injury with less permanent damage.

Origami DVD

Imagine being able to fold up your DVD player like a piece of paper and take it with you. You might be able to, if the e-paper DVD player becomes a reality! E-paper—a flexible screen that's as thin as a sheet of paper—is currently in development.

INDEX

A

airplane 73, 78–79, 81
alphabet 18–19, 57
animals 5, 9, 13, 22, 26, 52, 60
antibiotics 59, 63
Apple 87, 89
Archimedes 15, 16–17, 49

B

bacteria 37, 46, 47, 63
bathroom 28–29
battery 44–45, 55, 57, 83, 94
Bell, Alexander Graham 70, 71, 72–73
Bessemer, Henry 43
bronze 21, 28, 42

C

Cai Lun 26, 27
calculators 39, 85
camera 50, 51
canning, food 46–47
cars 34, 43, 45, 67, 68–69, 87
catapult 17, 49
cell phones 48, 71, 73
Cerf, Vinton 90, 91
China 9, 13, 20, 23, 25, 26, 27, 29, 32, 48, 57, 62
cities 15, 49, 57, 69
clocks 11, 35, 38–39
clothing 8, 9, 22, 23, 27
compass 24–25, 52
computer 45, 65, 71, 84–87, 88, 89, 90, 91
cuneiform 18, 20

D

da Vinci, Leonardo 34–35
doctors 59, 62, 63

E

Edison, Thomas 55, 60, 61, 75, 93
Egypt 16, 19, 21, 26, 28, 50, 57, 63
electricity 31, 44, 45, 52, 53, 55, 61, 71, 73, 76, 77

electric battery see battery
electric motor 52–53, 55
electromagnetism 53, 55, 57
energy 41, 45, 53, 55, 66, 67, 77
engine 15, 40–41, 66–67, 79, 81, 82, 84
Europe 4, 13, 19, 23, 25, 26, 33, 39, 47, 50, 54

F

factories 23, 31, 41, 47, 53, 59, 61, 69, 82
Faraday, Michael 25, 53, 54–55
farming 7, 12, 13, 15, 31
Farnsworth, Philo 76, 77
fertilizers 15, 58–59
food 5, 7, 12, 13, 31, 46, 47, 58, 59, 82, 83
Ford, Henry 69
France 35, 47, 49, 51, 69
Franklin, Benjamin 45, 52

G

Galilei, Galileo 37, 39, 62
Gates, Bill 87, 88–89
gears 11, 14, 15, 35
government 7, 15, 27, 31, 49, 56
Great Britain 41, 43, 47, 53, 57, 59, 75, 77, 85
Greek 15, 16, 19, 33, 40, 49, 50
Gutenberg, Johann 32, 33

I

Industrial Revolution 23, 31, 41, 53, 81
Internet 71, 73, 90–91
iron 7, 20, 41, 42, 43, 45, 58, 61, 81
Italy 28, 34, 35, 45, 67, 75

J

Jobs, Steve 87, 88–89

K

kitchen 82–83

L

language 19, 72, 73, 85
Latin 19, 50
lenses 17, 34, 36–37, 51, 55
light bulb 60–61

M

magnet 25, 53
Marconi, Guglielmo 55, 74, 75
medicine 59
Mesopotamia 7, 10, 11, 13, 15, 20, 26, 32
messages 56, 57, 70, 74, 75, 91
microscope 37
Microsoft 87, 89
microwave 83
Morse code 57, 73, 75
MP3 92–93
MS-DOS 87, 89
music 34, 91, 93

N

needle 8–9

P

paper 26–27, 29, 33, 45, 51, 57, 63, 65, 83, 85
Parkes, Alexander 80, 81
pasteurization 47
personal computer 86–87
photograph 50–51
plastic 62, 80–81
plow 12–13
pottery 10
printing press 32–33, 37

R

radio 55, 74–75
roads 11, 69
rubber 20, 49, 73, 80

S

school 20–21, 38, 89
shadouf 14
spinning wheel 22–23
steam engine 40–41, 66, 82, 84
steel 5, 13, 31, 42–43, 81, 82

T

telegraph 56–57, 70, 73, 75, 76, 80
telephone 57, 70–71, 73, 91
telescope 37
television 76–77
textiles 23, 41
thermometer 62
tools 43, 48
trade 7, 15, 19, 37, 39
trains 43

U

United States 21, 61, 71, 77, 79, 85, 87, 91

V

vacuum tubes 75, 77, 85
Volta, Alessandro 44, 45, 52, 55

W

war 47, 48–49, 56
water pump 14–15
water screw 15, 16
weapons 42, 43, 48, 49, 59
wheel 10–11, 14, 15, 23, 48, 82
Whitney, Eli 69
World Wide Web 91
Wright, Orville and Wilbur 78, 79
writing 7, 15, 18, 19, 20, 27, 33, 48, 89

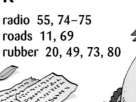